Gavin & Stacey

Gavin & Stacey

From Barry to Billericay

James Corden and Ruth Jones

HarperCollins*Publishers*

rry Island

HarperCollins*Publishers*
77–85 Fulham Palace Road,
Hammersmith, London W6 8JB
www.harpercollins.co.uk

Cover design © HarperCollins*Publishers*
Designed throughout by unreal
www.unreal-uk.com

First published by HarperCollins 2008

10 9 8 7 6 5 4 3 2 1

Edited by The Dawson Brothers

A catalogue record of this book is
available from the British Library

ISBN-13 978-0-00-729257-8
ISBN-10 0-00-729257-0

Printed and bound in Italy by
Rotolito Lombarda

DISCLAIMER: THIS IS A WORK OF FICTIONAL HUMOUR. ALL CHARACTERS, INCIDENTS AND EVENTS ARE THE PRODUCT OF THE AUTHORS' IMAGINATION. REFERENCES TO REAL PERSONS, PLACES OR EVENTS ARE MADE IN A FICTIONAL CONTEXT FOR ENTERTAINMENT PURPOSES, AND ARE NOT INTENDED TO BE IN ANY WAY FACTUAL.

Picture Credits:

Photographs on pages 16, 20, 26, 30/1, 34, 38/39, 44/5, 46/7, 48/9, 56, 94, 97, 106/7, 140/1, 200/1 © Baby Cow Productions

Photographs on pages 12, 28, 58/9, 62/3, 64/5, 68/9, 70/1, 72/3, 74/5, 76/7, 139, 160/1 © Adrian Rogers

Photographs on pages 10, 15, 18/19, 27, 29, 31, 36/7, 41, 52, 60, 66/7, 100/1, 101/2, 114/5, 136/7, 170/1 © Niel Bennett

Photographs on pages 94–7 courtesy of Hilary and Andrew Philips at Island Leisure

p. iv–v, 214-215 (maps) © HarperCollins Publishers; pp. 17 (roses), 40 (Severn Bridge), 41 (Cardiff), 52, 53, 79 (Stonehenge), 105 (golf clubs), 108-109 (Severn Bridge), 124, 125, 126, 127, 137 (omelette, right), 147 (rabbit in hat), 171 (pager) © iStockphoto.com; pp. 50-51 (map of world), 80-81, 96 (amusement arcade), 106-107 (mobile phones), 157 (cigars), 196, 197, 198, 199, 207 © Shutterstock.com; p. 114 (Charles and Camilla) © Samir Hussein/WireImage/Getty Images; p. 160 (left) © Dave M. Benett/Getty Images; p.160 (middle) © Jean Baptiste Lacroix/WireImage/Getty Images; p. 160 (right) © Dave Fisher/Rex Features; p. 161 (left) © Zhu Llangcheng/ChinaFotoPress/Getty Images; p. 161 (middle) ITV/Rex Features; p. 161 (right) © Action Press/Rex Features.

FACEBOOK® is a registered trade mark of Facebook Inc. Facebook webpage designs © Facebook Inc. 2008.

Bebo profile © Copyright 2008 Bebo

iTunes is a trademark of Apple Inc. iTunes webpage layout/'Content' – copyright © 2008 Apple Inc. All rights reserved.

Bad – performed by Michael Jackson. Composer Michael J. Jackson, Lyricist Michael J. Jackson. (P) 1987 MJJ Productions Inc. © 1987 Mijac Music (BMI) All rights on behalf of Mijac Music administered by Warner-Tamerlane Publishing Corp. Published By: Warner-Tamerlane Publishing Corp / Mijac Music.

Better Together – performed and written by Jack Johnson (2005), published by Bubble Toes Publishing / Universal Music Corp. (ASCAP).

When You Say Nothing At All – performed by Ronan Keating (1999). Written by Don Schlitz and Paul L Overstreet. Published by MCA Music Publishing, A.D.O. Universal Studio / Don Schlitz Music /Screen-Gems EMI Music Inc / Scarlett Moon Music Inc. / Roba /Universal MCA Music Publishing.

Wise Men – performed by James Blunt (2005). Written by J Blunt, S Skarbek, A Ghost. Published by Bucks Music Group Ltd / EMI Music Publishing / Universal Music Corp.

BBC logo is copyright and trademark of the British Broadcasting Corporation and is used under licence. BBC logo © BBC 1996.

Mr & Mrs logo and format produced under licence for 2waytraffic and ©2008 2waytraffic. All rights reserved. By arrangement with Derek Batey Enterprises Ltd.

GLC logo provided by kind permission of Goldie Lookin Chain and Metropolis Music.

Thanks to Crimestoppers and Barry Island Pleasure Park for their assistance with this book.

Foreword

Well, this is peachy. Look at me now – sat here at my desk writing what to all intents and purposes is an email (that's an electronic letter). And I'm sending it to my book publishers! I know!! Mr Harper and Mrs Collins – they're not a couple, and nor is Mrs Collins Jackie Collins as I first thought. It's just a coincidence.

So they've asked me to write a page about this book. I won't call it *my* book – because it's *everyone's* book. I'm just the glue if you will, the chef! Mixing all the ingredients – a bit like Hugh Fearnley-Whittingstall. Or Mick!

Essentially what it is, is a collection of the family's bits and bobs – a bit of Barry Bric and Billericay Brac. Ooh, that's a tongue-twister! (If you're expecting a book full of tongue-twisters then I should point out you might be disappointed.) But no – it's things about our family, it is! The Shipmans' and the Wests' – things that I thought you would like to read. And don't feel you're being invasive or nosy by reading it, because we're a very open lot and we like to share. If there's one thing people say about a Shipman or a West, it's that they've got nothing to hide.

So that's it, I'm signing off. I can waste no more time with this – I've given it my all. And if you're buying this as a gift for someone else and you fancy a little flick-through beforehand then go for it! I promise not to tell a soul, hee hee!

All the best,

Bryn

P.S. If anyone is looking for a Welsh translation of the above, then please contact Dic Powell at dpowell@dicpowell.co.uk.

From: staceywest@bedmoreelectronics.co.uk

Subject: Order No. 47646

To: gavin.shipman@icb-systems.co.uk

Mr Shipman,

Neil Barker has asked me to email you with regards to your ongoing order No.47646 (Thermal Fins). We just wanted to clarify your supply requirements over the next two months.

Kind Regards,

Ms. Stacey West
Sales Assistant
Bedmore Electronics

From: gavin.shipman@icb-systems.co.uk

Subject: Re: Order No. 47646

To: staceywest@bedmoreelectronics.co.uk

Ms West,

Many thanks for your email regarding order No. 47646. I can confirm that we will require 1000 Thermal Fins this month, then 1500 the following month.

Regards,

Gavin Shipman
ICB Systems

From: staceywest@bedmoreelectronics.co.uk

Subject: Re: Re: Order No. 47646

To: gavin.shipman@icb-systems.co.uk

Mr Shipman,

Thank you for your confirmation of Thermal Fin quantities over the next two months. I will update our delivery schedule accordingly.

Kind Regards,

Ms. Stacey West
Sales Assistant
Bedmore Electronics

From: gavin.shipman@icb-systems.co.uk

Subject: Re: Re: Re: Order No. 47646

To: staceywest@bedmoreelectronics.co.uk

Ms West,

Apologies for the inconvenience, but if it's not too late, we would like to increase our order from 1500 Thermal Fins next month up to 1750 units. Please let me know if this is possible.

Regards,

Gavin Shipman
ICB Systems

From: staceywest@bedmoreelectronics.co.uk

Subject: Re: Re: Re: Re: Order No. 47646

To: gavin.shipman@icb-systems.co.uk

Gavin,

I'm glad to say that it's not too late to change next month's order. We will deliver 1750 Thermal Fins next month as requested.

Kind Regards,

Stacey

PS. I hope this doesn't sound stupid, but what is a Thermal Fin?

From: gavin.shipman@icb-systems.co.uk

Subject: Re: Re: Re: Re: Re: Order No. 47646

To: staceywest@bedmoreelectronics.co.uk

Stacey,

Good question!! I don't know myself to be honest. I just got told we need 1750 of them next month! I'll try and find out...

Best wishes,

Gavin

From: gavin.shipman@icb-systems.co.uk

Subject: Re: Re: Re: Re: Re: Re: Order No. 47646

To: staceywest@bedmoreelectronics.co.uk

Stacey,

I just asked a geeky guy in our office called Eddie. He looked at me like I was an idiot then explained that Thermal Fins are like little blades which they put in computers to keep the parts cool. So now we know!

Best wishes,

Gavin

From: staceywest@bedmoreelectronics.co.uk

Subject: Re: Re: Re: Re: Re: Re: Re: Order No. 47646

To: gavin.shipman@icb-systems.co.uk

Gavin,

Oh God! I hope you didn't make yourself look stupid just 'cos of me!
Little fans, eh? Given that you lot seem so keen to get your hands on 1750!!! of them this month, I was hoping the answer would be a bit more exciting than that.

Kind Regards,

Stace

From: gavin.shipman@icb-systems.co.uk

Subject: Re: Re: Re: Re: Re: Re: Re: Re: Order No. 47646

To: staceywest@bedmoreelectronics.co.uk

Stace,

'More exciting than that'? Are you saying my job is boring? The cheek of it!
Well if my job's boring then yours must be too!

Gavin

From: staceywest@bedmoreelectronics.co.uk

Subject: Re: Re: Re: Re: Re: Re: Re: Re: Re: Order No. 47646

To: gavin.shipman@icb-systems.co.uk

Mr Shipman,

I'm so sorry that I offended you by suggesting that your job is boring. I hope you understand that I did not mean to cause you any distress. I hope that this apology means that you won't feel you have to contact Neil Barker to complain about my actions.

Yours sincerely

Ms Stacey West

From: gavin.shipman@icb-systems.co.uk

Subject: Re: Re: Re: Re: Re: Re: Re: Re: Re: Re: Order No. 47646

To: staceywest@bedmoreelectronics.co.uk

```
What's your phone number?
```

From: staceywest@bedmoreelectronics.co.uk

Subject: Re: Re: Re: Re: Re: Re: Re: Re: Re: Re: Re: Order No. 47646

To: gavin.shipman@icb-systems.co.uk

01632 960 991

From: staceywest@bedmoreelectronics.co.uk

Subject: Thanks!

To: gavin.shipman@icb-systems.co.uk

Gavin,

God, thanks so much for calling just now! As I said, I thought you were genuinely annoyed that I called your job boring. Cacking myself, I was! Now I've spoken to you and heard what you're like, I can totally see that you were just having a laugh!
It's funny talking to you 'cos reading your emails, I thought you'd sound a bit like Jude Law. But you sound more like a cockney in real life!

Stace

From: gavin.shipman@icb-systems.co.uk

Subject: Re: Thanks!

To: staceywest@bedmoreelectronics.co.uk

```
First she calls me boring, then she calls me a cockney! Honestly. We're not
all cockneys in south England you know...I'm from Billericay! That makes
me an Essex boy thank you very much.

Gav

PS - You're not the only one who thinks my job is boring. My best mate
Smithy banned me from talking to him about work after my first day
here.
```

From: staceywest@bedmoreelectronics.co.uk

Subject: Re: Re: Re: Thanks!

To: gavin.shipman@icb-systems.co.uk

Gav,

Sounds like your mate Smithy and me might get on! I bet he doesn't know what a Thermal Fin is either – is he single!??? Joking I am! And anyway I'm not sure a long-distance Essex/Wales relationship would have worked out!

Any nice plans for the weekend?

Stace

From: gavin.shipman@icb-systems.co.uk

Subject: Re: Re: Re: Re: Thanks!

To: staceywest@bedmoreelectronics.co.uk

```
Me, Smithy and the boys are going to Ritzy's for foam night. Smithy
loves a foam party! I used to as well, but these days I get fed up of all
the soap on my going-out clothes. Still, it'll be a good laugh. I'll put
some photos on facebook so you can see them on Monday. Look out for a
friend request...

Have a good one,

Gav
```

From: staceywest@bedmoreelectronics.co.uk

Subject: Foam Photos

To: gavin.shipman@icb-systems.co.uk

Oh my God! You lot were hammered on Saturday, weren't you? How funny! You look different to how I thought you would. I thought you'd be a bit more like Michael Caine when he was younger. That said, I've never seen Michael Caine at a foam party.

Stace

From: gavin.shipman@icb-systems.co.uk

Subject: Re: Foam Photos

To: staceywest@bedmoreelectronics.co.uk

```
Hey Stace,
Michael Caine? Well I hope I'm an improvement on that! I've just had a
look at your photos from the weekend. You look pretty hammered too, Mrs!
Obviously you Welsh girls can't take your drink. I'd love to see how your
lot would do in a drinking competition with my lot.

Gav
```

From: staceywest@bedmoreelectronics.co.uk

Subject: Re: Foam Photos

To: gavin.shipman@icb-systems.co.uk

We'd drink you Essex boys under the table! You know what? Us taffs would beat you lot at almost anything. Just watch – our boys will hammer yours in the Grand Slam at the weekend. £20 says we will do you.

Stace

From: gavin.shipman@icb-systems.co.uk

Subject: Re: Foam Photos

To: staceywest@bedmoreelectronics.co.uk

```
Do me? I don't like the sound of the Welsh rugby team doing me for £20!!
But you're on. You better go to the cashpoint now so you can have it in
the post first thing Monday.

Gav

PS. Give me your mobile number so I can send you a gloating text after
the match.
PPS. I promise not to send you dirty text messages
PPPS. ...until next week
```

From: staceywest@bedmoreelectronics.co.uk

Subject: £20

To: gavin.shipman@icb-systems.co.uk

I told you we'd do it! You better get that £20 in the post fast.

Stace

PS. You broke your promise! I could have you up on an industrial tribunal on that text evidence alone!!!

From: gavin.shipman@icb-systems.co.uk

Subject: Re: £20

To: staceywest@bedmoreelectronics.co.uk

```
Whatever. I don't even like rugby. It's just posh boys groping each other.
I'm a football man. And believe me, Wales will never beat us at that. We
would whip you.

Anyway, fair's fair. I owe you £20. The only thing is, I'm not very
comfortable posting cash - it might get stolen. I'd feel much better if
I could give it to you in person. Are you coming over here with Neil for
the meeting next week?

Gav
```

From: staceywest@bedmoreelectronics.co.uk

Subject: Re: Re: £20

To: gavin.shipman@icb-systems.co.uk

I'm not coming to Billericay for that meeting with Neil. I never get to leave the office, me! I agree though. Money does get stolen in the post, so we probably should just meet up. I've had a look at a map and half way between you and me is Swindon. We could meet there. You could bring Smithy along and I can bring my mate Nessa – it'd be a right laugh! And you can give me the £20.

As you're English and Swindon's in England you probably know more about where's good to go out there. Any ideas?

Stace

From: gavin.shipman@icb-systems.co.uk

Subject: Re: Re: Re: £20

To: staceywest@bedmoreelectronics.co.uk

```
I looked up good places to go out in Swindon on the internet and nothing
came up. So how about we meet up in London instead? We could go out in
the West End! Smithy's up for it - he's intrigued as to which one Nessa
is on your Facebook photos.

Gav
```

From: staceywest@bedmoreelectronics.co.uk

Subject: Re: Re: Re: Re: £20

To: gavin.shipman@icb-systems.co.uk

West End – that sounds lush! We could go to Leicester Square and see if there are any film premieres going on. Maybe Tom Cruise will phone up my mum! Oh, and I'm afraid Nessa banned me from putting any photos of her on facebook for legal reasons.
I know it's a bit short notice – but what about doing it this Saturday?

Stace
X X

From: gavin.shipman@icb-systems.co.uk

Subject: Re: Re: Re: Re: Re: £20

To: staceywest@bedmoreelectronics.co.uk

```
Saturday? Amazing! Let's do it! I'm definitely up for it. How about
we meet in the middle of Leicester Square, then we can go and get
pissed somewhere. And I can get the first round in with that £20
I owe you - though that'll only get you two drinks in London!

I can't wait!

Gav

X X

PS - We need another 1750 Thermal Fins next month.
```

ICB SYSTEMS

EMPLOYEE
Gavin Shipman

COMMUNICATION SKILLS
Gavin is a very patient employee. He often has to talk to Tracy (I believe that's her name) at Bedmore's. She can stay on the phone for hours, yet he's very good at dealing with that. He appears to charm her into getting the parts. This shows very strong personal skills.

IT EQUIPMENT SKILLS
Gavin certainly knows his way round the computer system. He probably receives the most client e-mails of anyone in the company. A very talented lad.

TIME MANAGEMENT
Gavin is very good at keeping to deadlines. Although recently he has taken a lot of holiday. It appears he's doing short day breaks. He's also been sick quite a lot lately – particularly after he ran out of flexidays. The temp we got to replace him has done very well at dealing with senior clients and is very good at dealing directly with Tracy's line-manager, Neil (Tracy has been off on many of the days that the temp was working).

ENERGY, DETERMINATION AND WORK-RATE
When he is in the office Gavin is a very hard worker; very little slows him down. We recently had an incident with one of Gavin's friends disrupting the work place by bursting into tears. It was something to do with a schoolgirl – presumably the guy's daughter. We weren't very happy about this, but he managed to confine the whole incident to his lunch-break. So no problems there.

ICB SYSTEMS

DELEGATION SKILLS

Gavin is very good at delegation. You'll often hear him say 'That's not my problem', and that's why he's so efficient at his job. If it's nothing to do with him then he's happy to pass it on to others. It would be even better if the other people in the office thought the same.

OVERALL

Gavin's excellent client relationships make him a great asset to the company. The only minus for Gavin is that he's a Spurs fan! Seriously though, that isn't a real minus. ICB do not condone discrimination of any kind.

Signed and dated by appraisee:

Gavin Shipman   01-05-08

Signed and dated by appraiser:

01-05-08

STACEY SHIPMAN
7 LIME TREE AVENUE
BILLERICAY

Dear Chelmsford Zoo, attached is my application for the position of reptile administration assistant. Yours, Stacey Shipman.

PROFILE:

I have good people skills – because I have worked with people a lot in all my jobs. More importantly for this job, I also have good animal skills. For example, cats always come to me for some reason. I think I must have been a cat in a previous life or something. I think I'd be fine with reptiles.

If you employ me I promise that I will definitely always try my hardest. I am trustworthy, conscientious, empathic, confident, efficient, talented and modest. I'm very good with money too. And I've also developed very good problem-solving skills – I can usually beat solitaire on hard and I attained the office high-score at Mine Sweeper in my last job.

I'm very keen to get a job because staying at home waiting for Gav is, to be honest, dead boring.

MAJOR ACHIEVEMENTS:

– Redlund Logistics Employee of the Day (Sept 11th 2001)
– Won 2nd place at the Brain of Barry pub quiz. (Team Work)
– I once paraglided in Greece. That was pretty immense.
– I can lick my elbow. Not many of my friends can do that.

CAREER HISTORY:

Various Projects, 2007–current
I am currently taking a career break to find myself as well as picking up new skills. And what better place to do it than from home. I've also developed a keen interest in Boxercise.

Sales Assistant, Bedmore's Electronics, 2004–2007
I spent a lot of my time working the phones. Once I got them working I spend a lot of time on the phones. I would say that I'm very persistent – I was once on the phone for over two hours to a computer company I regularly deal with just to sort out one order. The company showed me the phone records after, so they definitely have them. I also pride myself in picking up lots of company knowledge – particularly in and around the kitchen, water cooler, smoking area and toilet.

The skills picked up from this job were:
– Looking up part numbers
– Copying part numbers from books in to computers and vice versa
– Phone and communication skills
– Internet and email skills
– Organizational skills (incl. Christmas pub trip & Sandra's birthday pub trip)

Admin Assistant, Redlund Logistics, 2001–2004
I was responsible for noting down when the drivers came in, when they went out and what the drivers were transporting – all of which I noted in to the computer system. It was here that I developed my strong estimational skills for when I forgot to enter the data. This was also a great place for developing my phone manner. Although I wasn't technically supposed to use the phone, I used my interpersonal skills to talk the office manager guy in to giving me one.

Gap Year, 2000–2001
I spent a lot of my time educating myself about all the different places in the world. Unfortunately I never quite got around to going to any of them. However, I did spend a lot of my time in town improving my interpersonal skills and my purchasing skills.

Service, Tony the Grocer's, 1999–2000
I'll be honest, I didn't really enjoy being a grocer. Not Tony's fault. It wasn't my calling. And it was just too much like hard work. I would come home at the end of the day and my back would be aching. The plums were on the floor, see? And the pears were dead high up. So I was up and down all the time. Like a yo-yo I was. Very tiring.

REFEREES:

SANDRA JONES (Head of Accounts)
Bedmore Electronics
Barry Industrial Estate
Barry Island
Wales

NESSA JENKINS (Head of Finance)
Barry Island Pleasure Park
Barry Island
Wales

Stacey's

How To Make Personal Phone Calls At Work Without Being Noticed

I quite frequently got warned about making personal phone calls / texts / e-mails on work time, particularly to Gav. But how else am I supposed to pass the day? That's why I developed a series of techniques I used to stop myself getting told off.

MAKE FRIENDS WITH YOUR CLIENTS

You're not allowed to talk to friends, but you are allowed to talk to clients. That's how your company makes money, isn't it? Perfect! To make the situation even better you might even get to date a client, in which case you would be obliged to talk to your boyfriend. Plus you can spend ages on the phone to him without having to pay the bill. Leaving your mobile minutes for some more chatting after work.

TOILET TEXT

If work's getting you down then take a toilet break. Once you've locked yourself in a cubicle, they can't get you. At this point you can text to your heart's content. Key factors to getting away with this are: 1. Turn off the key pressing sounds on your mobile and 2. If anyone comes in either stop texting or press the keys slower, so they don't make quiet clicking sounds. A rapid series of clicks would give the game away instantly. The added bonus to this system is no one can ever have a go at you for it. I mean, who's going to comment on how long you were in the lav for? And anyway, as far as they're concerned, you were probably just doing your business in there as all of us have to do.

MAKE FRIENDS, NOT ENEMIES

It's very important to have everyone in the office on side. Muck around with them, and make them feel like you really get on. That way they will be much more forgiving when you waste time at work. The most important person to keep sweet is the IT guy. He's the one who can see who you're emailing. So try to spend a lot of time flirting with him. If he starts talking about networks and processes, just nod as if you know what he means, even though you don't. If you can, explain to him how there's a funny clip on Youtube that you'd really like to show him. That way he'll let you access that website – which is pretty immense 'cos no-one else in the office has access to that.

MAKE IT A HABIT

If you're the sort of person who rarely call friends from work then you will be spotted as soon as you try to do so. So this is how you get round that. On the first day of a new job just get straight on the phone and start contacting loads of your mates. Properly take the piss. Then, when they tell you off, you can say 'Sorry, I'll keep the personal calls to a minimum'. They'll be grateful that you are making the effort, and so when you only spend 30 minutes on the phone to a friend they'll be all 'Thanks for not spending more time on the phone!'. Dead easy.

EXCUSES

If any of these techniques fail and you do get in trouble you can try the following excuses:

"I didn't send that e-mail. My machine must have some sort of virus."

"I worked till 18.25 last night, and that call was 25 minutes. I'm just taking back the time I earned yesterday."

"It was a txt from head office."

"We were talking business. Although what were talking about was our own business."

If your boss is male:

"I was talking to my friend about my women's problems."

Stacey's

Questionnaire: How To Find Out If This Is 'The One'

Answer the following questions (truthfully) to see whether or not your new man really is the one for you, or whether he's just another numpty who'll probably end up nothing more than an ex-fiancé.

Q1 What sort of clothes does he wear?
a) Fashionable and sexy
b) Whatever his mum's chosen that morning
c) Standard issue prison overalls

Q2 He asks about where you live. Do you...?
a) Get very excited – he's obviously interested in you
b) Tell him it's shit to disuade him from visiting – you don't want your friends seeing him
c) Give him a false address. And name. And phone number. Then set off your rape alarm

Q3 You've taken him to meet your friends and family. Does Uncle Bryn...?
a) Say he reminds him of Achmed
b) Say he reminds him of Leighton
c) Say nothing at all – he's stopped speaking to you

Q4 What was the last thing he gave you?
a) A rose
b) A rose he stole from a grave yard.
c) An STD

Q5 In conversation does he...
a) Ask you lots of questions?
b) Talk about himself?
c) Burp the names of his favourite prostitutes?

Q6 Your mobile phone beeps in the middle
of the night with a new text –
it could be from 'him'. Do you..?
a) Go all tingly and rush
to see what it says
b) Decide to look at it in the morning,
roll over and go back to sleep
c) Press 'delete' before you've opened it
in case he's got read-receipts
turned on

Q7 Has he told his mates about you?
a) Yeah! They know more about
me than I do!
b) I can't tell 'cos he won't let
me meet them
c) Yes, but he texted them a
topless picture of you.

Q8 If he dumped you
tomorrow, would you...?
a) Be heartbroken and unable to leave
the house for weeks
b) Start missing your steamy bedroom
sessions with him
c) Go out and celebrate with Nessa

Q9 When did he first say 'I love you'...?
a) First date
b) Still waiting...
c) To a photo in Nuts magazine.

Q10 Does the thought of spending the rest
of your life with him make you feel?
a) All warm and fuzzy
b) Nervous
c) Suicidal

ANSWERS

☆ *Mostly As* – This is definitely
'the one'. Marry him now!

☆ *Mostly Bs* – He sounds
lush but is it enough? You could
propose, but it's probably best
you stick to hanky-panky and the
occasional meal on neutral territory.

☆ *Mostly Cs* – What are you
thinking? This bloke sounds like
a right weirdo. Leave. Now.

Either all As, all Bs or all Cs – You're
becoming OCD. You really need to get
out more.

HYWEL

LOOKS	★★★★★★★★☆☆
WEALTH	★★★★★★★★★★
MORALITY	★★★★★★★★★☆
PROXIMITY	★★★★★★★★★★
PROS	FIRST LOVE
CONS	MISSING TEETH

KYLE

LOOKS	★★★★★★★★☆☆
TWAT LEVEL	★★★★★★★★★★
FAMILY	★★★★★★★★★★
PROXIMITY	★★★★★★★★★★
PROS	FAMILY TREAT US LIKE ROYALTY
CONS	A PRICK

LEIGHTON

LOOKS	★★★★★★★★★☆
ARROGANCE	★★★★★★★★★★★★★
MORALITY	★★★★★★★★☆☆
PROXIMITY	★★★★★★★★★★
PROS	STRONG AT MATHS
CONS	IF HE WAS CHOCOLATE HE'D EAT HIMSELF

ACHMED

LOOKS	★★★★★★☆☆☆☆
NICENESS	★★★★★★★★★☆
WEALTH	★★★★★★★☆☆☆
PROXIMITY	★★★★★★★★★★
	★★★★★ SWINDON
PROS	ALWAYS SENDS BRYN A CHRISTMAS CARD
CONS	JUST TOO NICE

CLIFFORD

LOOKS	★★★★★★★★★☆
WEALTH	★★★★★★★★★★
MORALITY	★★★★★★★★★★
PROXIMITY	★★★★★★★★★★
PROS	ENTREPRENEURIAL, CRACKING-LOOKING
CONS	DOESN'T GET OUT TILL 2034

GAVIN

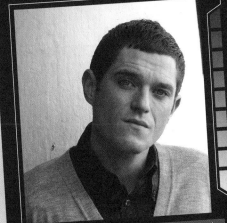

LOOKS	★★★★★★★★★★
WEALTH	★★★★★★★☆☆☆
ROMANCE	★★★★★★★★★★
PROXIMITY	★☆☆☆☆☆☆☆☆☆
PROS	MY SOUL MATE!
CONS	LIVES BLOODY MILES AWAY

facebook

home   account   privacy   logout

Search

Applications edit

- Photos
- Groups
- Marketplace
- Events
- Superprod!
- Likeness
- Friends GPS

Share you photos with friends on Facebook

Profile edit   Friends ▼   Inbox ▶

Stacey Shipman
just had a brunch!

Updated on Monday edit

View photos of Stacey (197)

View Stacey's Friends (110)

Prod Stacey

Throw a sheep at Stacey

▶ **Information**

Networks:	Essex
Sex:	Female
Relationship status	Married to Gavin West
Hometown:	Barry Island

Interests: Gavin West, Judith Chalmers boxercise, White Wine Spritzers, made-for-TV movies. (There's loads more, but I'll be honest I can't think what they might be.)

Favourite Music: Take That (our wedding song), Goldie Lookin' Chain (Go Wales!), Gareth Gates (not the music), Charlotte Church (not the presenting)

Favourite TV Shows: Big Brother. But I always forget to watch it; they should advertise it more. Cash in the Attic. Loose Women. I never got the title – everyone on it always seems so uptight.

To be honest I'll watch anything that's on. The other week I even watched a documentary on custard, it was actually dead interesting. I do worry about myself sometimes.

Favourite Movies: Harry Potter and the Philosopher's Stone, Harry Potter and the Chamber of Secrets, Harry Potter and the Goblet of Fire. I'm not very good at thinking under pressure. But I do like them all though.

Favourite Books: A Brief History of Time (only joking). The Naked Chef (I often read it and imagine what the food might taste like), The Da Vinci Code (not read it, but the cover's good and I liked the film)

Favourite Quotes: 'You are now pronounced man and wife.' Father Chris, 2007

'And punch it out and do it again, and do it again.' Judith Chalmers, 2006

'You've met me half way on the rape alarm... so if you come back Sunday, raped, and I showed you how to use it, I'll rest easy in my bed. You come back on Sunday raped, the fault will lie solely at your door.' Uncle Bryn, 2007 (He really is a very loving man)

▶ **Friends**
87 friends   See all

Nessa

Jason

Mum

▶ **Photos**
1 of 14 albums   See all

Wedding pics

More Wedding pics

▼ The Wall

Import | See all

Write something on your own wall...

Post

Bryn West (Barry) wrote at 11.32pm

Did you get the present I sent you? It was a hotdog. I sent it because you mentioned being hungry this morning. It's not actually a real hot dog, but a small photo of one. I really hope you did get it 'cos that tiny picture cost 1$ (£0.508)!

Gavin Shipman (Billericay) wrote at 3.24pm

I saw that you had brunch again this morning which got me thinking – what are we having for dupper (dinner/supper) tonight?

Bryn West (Barry) wrote at 11.32pm

I think I accidentally 'super prodded' you earlier. I pressed the button without meaning to. I think my mouse might be malfunctioning. It's one of those cordless ones with the red light on the bottom. It sort of jumps around a lot. I much preferred the one with the little ball on the bottom. You knew where you were with that.

Doris (Barry) wrote at 9.38am on June 10th, 2007

Did you and your fella try out any of the things I messaged you about yesterday? I appreciate that you don't have any handcuffs – but you could just use strips of material and tie the hands up rather than cuff them.

▼ Groups

4 groups · See all · ✕

Daytime TV Addicts • Job Hunters Anonymous • Doris' Hot Men Appreciation Society • How Many Times Have You Done It To Cash In The Attic? • TV Star Mick Shipman's Fan Club. • Bryn's Best Omelettes Made By Gwen!

▼ Gifts

You have 4 gifts · Send a Gift · ✕

From Bryn

From Gavin

From Pam

▼ Daytime TV Trivia

Choose subject · See all · ✕

Stacey's

'Dear John' Letters

Dear Hywel,

Oh Hywel. This is the hardest thing I've ever had to put down on paper, this is. I'm cacking myself just writing it.

You know yesterday when you asked me if I could feel the 'electricity' between us, and how I hesitated before saying 'yes'? And you know how, when I talked about going to Torquay on holiday, I used the word 'I' rather than 'we'? And you know how we've always been great together? And how it's almost as if we're friends? Like best friends? Which would be a good thing? Yeah?

Well, and I want to be clear, I do think you are lush, but I don't think our feelings are quite in the same place, you know? Do you get what I'm saying? It's like you're a 'one' and I'm a 'one', but if you add us together we don't make a 'two' - if you follow? I think I've made it clear. I don't want any misunderstandings. So we're good, yeah?

Anyhow I'm so very, very, sorry.

All my love,
Stace
XoXoXoX

P.S. Is it OK to use 'and' at the start of sentences? I never can remember how to use them proper.

Dear Kyle,

You're a twat! It's over. That's right! It's in writing. Yes, you may have broken up with me 'first' last night but I'm breaking up with you 'officially' in this letter. Nessa always said you were a prick. I should have listened to her. For that matter, she also said you looked like a rapist. Whilst I'm being honest, she did also say that your small hands indicate that you have a tiny manhood. Which, although it's not true, is something to bear in mind. 'Cos other people might be thinking the same of you.

Anyway, I don't ever want to see you again! You've broken my heart. I thought you were my soul mate! You bastard!

I hate you!

Stacey

P.S. Bryn has just popped in - he wants me to ask if your family are well.

Dear Leighton,

Please read this through before you react. I've thought long and hard about this, and I don't think it's working between us. And I know I've said this before, but this time I mean it, I don't think we should see each other any more. I was in a bad place the last three times I said this, but I don't think I'm lying this time. I'm deadly serious. Honest.

And don't think this has anything to do with the engagement ring you got me - I appreciate that the metal ones are very expensive.

I do appreciate that I'm pulling out just days before the wedding, but that's got to be better than pulling out after the wedding, right? How bad would I be if I did that, eh? Anyhow, it's not like we can't still be friends.

Please don't be mad,
Stacey
XxX

Dear Clifford,

I think you'll appreciate my situation. You're in prison, I'm not. And that's not conducive for a close-knit family unit, is it?

You know what? I've written a few rejection letters in my time. So I'm just going to come out and say it. Cliff, I'm dumping you.

Good luck,
Stace XxX

P.S. Bryn made me enclose a couple of small bars of soap he stole whilst on holiday. He says that if you drop your soap in the shower now, there's no need to pick it up as you can just unwrap a new one.

Dear Achmed,

I can't do it Achmed. If you leave, I don't think I'm going to be able to follow you. I love Barry Island. I grew up here. My family and friends are here and I've got to be honest – I'm not a fan of Swindon. (Although Bryn has tried to convince me that it's worth going there for the 'Oasis' swimming pool as it has a wave machine and water slides. But, as I tell him, that's not a strong enough reason for me).

I apologize if you see your Facebook page before you get this letter. I happened to be online over lunch so I changed my relationship status to 'single' and I've already been emailed by a few of your friends asking me what happened. At least you won't have to keep repeating the news to your mates. That's a positive isn't it?

I'm so so sorry,
Stace
XxX

P.S. Bryn asked me to tell you that he misses you.

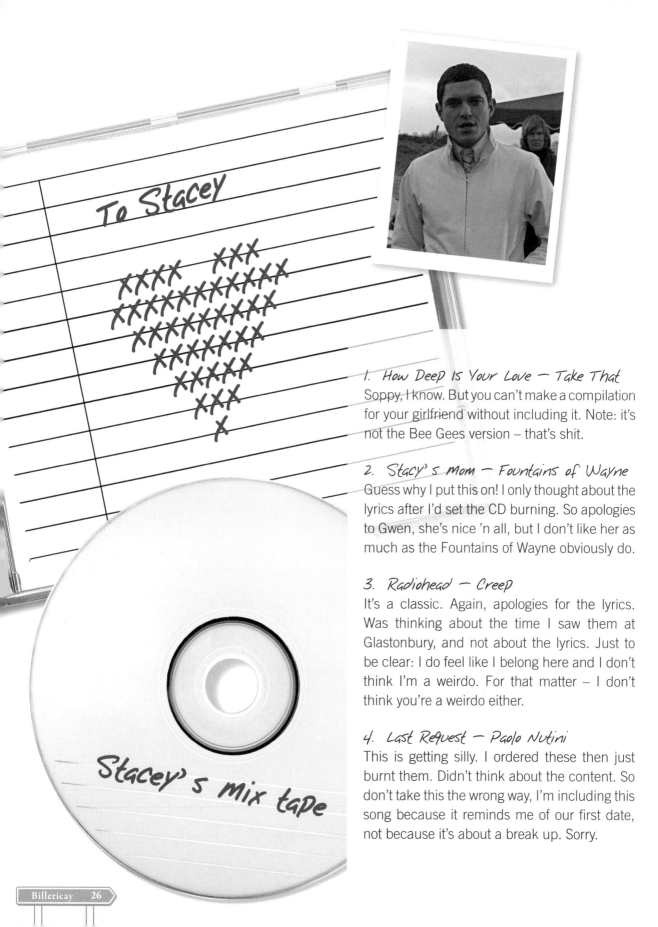

To Stacey

XXXX XXX
XXXXXXXXXXXXX
XXXXXXXXXXXX
XXXXXXXXXX
XXXXXXXX
XXXXXX
XXXX
X

Stacey's mix tape

1. How Deep Is Your Love — Take That
Soppy, I know. But you can't make a compilation for your girlfriend without including it. Note: it's not the Bee Gees version – that's shit.

2. Stacy's mom — Fountains of Wayne
Guess why I put this on! I only thought about the lyrics after I'd set the CD burning. So apologies to Gwen, she's nice 'n all, but I don't like her as much as the Fountains of Wayne obviously do.

3. Radiohead — Creep
It's a classic. Again, apologies for the lyrics. Was thinking about the time I saw them at Glastonbury, and not about the lyrics. Just to be clear: I do feel like I belong here and I don't think I'm a weirdo. For that matter – I don't think you're a weirdo either.

4. Last Request — Paolo Nutini
This is getting silly. I ordered these then just burnt them. Didn't think about the content. So don't take this the wrong way, I'm including this song because it reminds me of our first date, not because it's about a break up. Sorry.

5. Before I Fall to Pieces — Razorlight

This one's more like it. The lyrics don't make any particular sense. So hopefully nothing can be read into it. This was always on the radio at work the first time you called me, and so will forever make me think of you. Then again, Katie Price and Peter Andre's 'A Whole New World' was also on the radio a lot at the same time.

6. Prodigy — Out of Space

You can't fault the Prodigy. Good old Essex boys! You haven't seen dancing till you've seen Smithy dance to this. First time I saw it happen we thought the strobe lights at the leisure centre had given him a fit.

7. Suddenly — KT Tunstall

Every part of this song reflects how I feel about you, babe. Apart from the bit that says your face is like a map of the world. Your face just looks lovely. Not at all map-like.

8. Cutting Crew — I Just Died In Your Arms Tonight

There's nothing like an '80s power ballad. Particularly one that can marry death and love in the same breath. It's best to listen to the guitar solo (3:09) outside on a cliff on a windy day.

9. Ossie's Dream — 1980 81 Cup Final Squad with Chas 'n' Dave

Brilliant! They don't make songs like this anymore. I'm sure you've already got all the Chas 'n' Dave Spurs songs already though, haven't you! But just in case you haven't, this will complete your music collection.

10. Don't Look Back into the Sun — Libertines

Remember when you asked me what Pete Doherty did for a job? Well here's proof that he actually was a musician. Told you.

11. Mylo — In My Arms

I'm sure you'll know why I picked this one. It was our first kiss. It was good timing on our part – four minutes later and I'd have had to put Liberty X on here. Maybe that's why I made my move so quickly!

12. Could It Be Magic — Take That

I figured it could be a Take That sandwich. Okay, I'll be honest, I quite like Take That. But if you show this tape to anyone (particularly Smithy) I'll have to kill you.

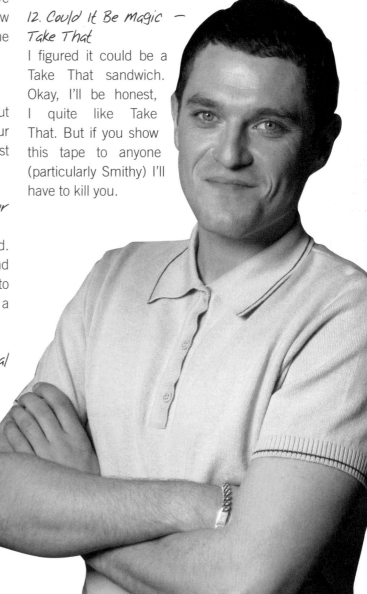

gav,

Thanks for your CD!!
I love it and have
listened to it loads!

Here's mine for you!

Love
Stace
xxx

gavin's Mixtape

1. A Million Love Songs - Take That
Seeing as you're such a big Take That fan, I thought I'd start with my favourite of theirs. You can listen to it while staring at your Gary Barlow posters!

2. Liberty X - A Little Bit More
Remember this? We had our second kiss to it! I used to hate this but now I think it's the lushest song ever!

3. Mousse T - Horny
Our third kiss! Could have been something a bit more romantic, couldn't it! That said, I don't think I'll ever forget the image of Smithy singing every single word of this at the top of his lungs.

4. James Blunt - You're Beautiful

I didn't mean to put this one on, but Bryn was mucking about with my playlist and must have added this on there. That's not to say you're not beautiful, though, Gav. You are!

5. Grease Medley - Unknown

Not my fault this one. A mixtape (or should that be mixCD!) isn't legal in these parts of South Wales if it doesn't have a Grease Medley on it. Out of my hands, it is. Just happens to be perfect for our girls nights out though!

6. Beyonce - Crazy In Love

I put this on 'cos I love this song and also 'cos I kind of think that you're my Beyonce and I'm your Jay-Z, I mean you're my Jay Z and I'm your Beyonce. Except you didn't used to be a drug dealer (to the best of my knowledge anyway) and I was never in Destiny's Child.

7. Robbie Williams - Angels

Forget Shakespeare, I honestly believe the words of this song are the most beautiful thing I've ever heard. I love the words so much that once, I nearly got them tattooed on my ankle. I'll be honest, I only changed my mind when Nessa said she didn't have anything to sterilize her needle with.

8. Gary Numan - Cars

Nessa's always playing this in the car (I've just realized how funny that sounds! She's playing 'Cars' in the car! It would be even more ridiculous if we were listening to it in Cardiff).

9. Will Young - Leave Right Now

Will Young is well lush. I voted for him ten times on Pop Idol. If I'm honest, I felt cheated when I found out he was gay. I never stood a chance, did I? Five quid wasted.

10. Amy Winehouse - Rehab

What a cracking voice she has. Do you really reckon she's a druggie like the papers are always saying? I can't see it myself. You couldn't have a voice like that AND look after that massive hairdo if you were off your face all the time, could you? Them tabloids are always making stuff up. Although did you hear about her beating up Wendy Richard? Unbelievable!

11. Rabbit - Chas 'n' Dave

I'd never heard of Chas 'n' Dave till you sent me your CD! They sound well funny – they sing like Smithy talks! To be a good girlfriend, I listened to some more of their songs and this one is probably my favourite. How on earth do they say 'Rabbit' so quickly? I've tried but I can't keep up.

12. Never Forget - Take That

A Take That sandwich for you too! Just like the boys say, I'll certainly never forget where I'm coming from! Once a Barry girl, forever a Barry girl!

facebook

Search

Applications edit

- Photos
- Groups
- Marketplace
- Events
- Superprod!
- Likeness
- Friends GPS

Share you photos with friends on Facebook

Profile edit   **Friends** | ▶   **Inbox** | ▶   home   account   privacy   logout

View photos of Gavin (197)

View Gavin's Friends (110)

Prod Gavin

Drop-kick Gavin

Gavin Shipman
is having steak tonight!

Updated on Monday edit

Networks:	Essex
Gender:	Male
Relationship status	Married to Stacey Shipman
Hometown:	Billericay

▼ **Information**

Interests: Tottenham Hotspur FC, Beers of the world, Stacey Shipman (in that order!!!)

Favourite Music: Take That (first time round), Prodigy (Essex boys!), Pussycat Dolls (Not the music)

Favourite TV Shows: Crimewatch. It's the only way I get to keep up with my old mates now I'm married!!!

10 O'Clock News, cos my Dad's in it!!!

Otherwise anything really - Sky Sports News, Gillette Soccer Saturday, Super Sunday, Soccer AM.

Favourite Movies: I like a whole range of stuff. From Godfather to Goodfellas, from Scarface to Casino.

Favourite Books: Nuts, Heat (I don't buy it though, I just read Stacey's)

▼ **Mini-Feed**

Displaying 4 stories   Import | See all

Yesterday

 Gavin wrote on Bryn's wall 11.53am Jan 25, 2008

The day before the day which was originally only two days before Today

 **Gavin commented on Stacey's picture**

▼ **The Wall**

▼ **Friends**

110 friends   See all

Budgie   Rudi   Bryn

▼ **Photos**

1 of 14 albums   See all

Write something on your own Wall

Post

Spurs Cup Final!

▼ **Groups**   ✕
4 groups   See all

I Love Ritzy's Foam Night • Billericay Olympic Bid 2020!!! • Smithstar's Pub Quiz • Bring back Chas'n'Dave • Make the Severn Bridge Toll a Nice Round Number • I'm a Man, I'm Not Gay, but I Still Like Take That

▼ **Gifts**   ✕
You have 4 gifts   Send a Gift

     From Pam Shipman

From Stacey

From Smithy

LITTLE DOUG (HM Prison Belmarsh) wrote at 4.52pm

Yeah. They do computer lessons every Thursday so we can get jobs when we get out. I spend most of my time on facebook. Can't get porn though. They've got filters, so don't email me any! Well, actually, you could always give it a try…

Pam Shipman (Billericay) wrote at 3.25pm on Jan 26, 2008

Dear son,

I've joined the 20th century and got myself on facebook! I've got two friends already – you and Bryn! You'll have to help me with putting pictures on when you get home. I'm having real trouble getting it all lined up properly and your Dad won't help 'cos he thinks it's a waste of time.
Lots of love,
Mum

P.S. Steak for tea.

Bryn West (Barry) wrote at 11.14am Jan 25, 2008

Watcha Gavin! I just thought I'd tell you that I've found a new 'facebook Application' which tells you what your Star Wars name is. Mine is Wesbr Hobar! Hilarious!

LITTLE DOUG (HM Prison Belmarsh) wrote at 3.25pm on Jan…

Gavlar! Long time no speak. Maybe that's because I'm in prison!!! How's Smithy and the boys?

Stacey Shipman (Barry) wrote at 9.38am on June 10th, 2007

I'm bored. What u doing? xxx

PS - Steak for tea :)

COSMOPOLITAN POLICE Working together for a safer London

WE·ARE APPEALING FOR WITNESSES
CAN YOU HELP US?

TERRORIST INCIDENT

THURS 22ND FEBRUARY 07 A MALE WITH
A SMALL PACKAGE JUMPED THE
TICKET BARRIER AT THIS STATION

In strictest confidence, please phone:

666 06 2400

DID YOU SEE OR HEAR ANYTHING?
PLEASE CALL US

On the number above at your local police station
Or ring the charity Crimestoppers anonymously

CRIMESTOPPERS
0800 555 111
Call anonymously with information about crime

COSMOPOLITAN POLICE

ATTACH

DATE OF INCIDENT	TIME (USE 2400 HOUR)	LOCATION
22 02 2007	1327	PADDINGTON STATION, PLATFORM 3

PERSONAL DETAILS

FORENAME(S)
GAVIN

SURNAME
SHIPMAN

ADDRESS
17 LIME TREE AVENUE, BILLERICAY, ESSEX

INCIDENT DESCRIPTION

At 0800 hours a young man was seen vaulting the ticket barrier carrying a tiny suspicious package. Station staff witnessed this breach of security regulations and, as he clearly looked a bit terrorist ey, they alerted members of the metropolitan police armed division. The suspect then sprinted down platform 3 with a glint in his eye (possibly evil) he then approached his female accomplice who was boarding a train. At this point, he produced the device, which he had secreted in a small bag. Our specially trained officers quickly identified this device as a dirty bomb and immediately trained their weapons on the suspect. He then uttered some romantic sounding codewords at which point the officers nullified the terrorist threat by wrestling him to the ground, thereby ensuring that the citizens of london could once again sleep safe in their beds.

SUSPECT'S CRIMINAL RECORD

YEAR	DESCRIPTION
2007	Traffic Offence (3 points) A12, Brentwood
2002	Indecent Exposure (Posterior) Billericay Town Centre

INCIDENT CONCLUSION

A subsequent ballistics inspection showed the suspect device was in actual fact an item of jewellery which had been purchased from the Paddington station branch of H.Samuel, and not a dirty bomb.

After questioning Mr Shipman overnight in the terrorist wing of Paddington Green Police Station, the Metropolitan Police decided not to prosecute him for suspected terrorist activities. But while it is well known the Metropolitan Police takes a tough stance on terrorism, it should also be noted that we take an equally tough stance on those who frequent railway platforms without being in possession of a valid ticket. For this reason, Mr Shipman felt the full force of the law when he was issued a maximum penalty of £15 for his crime.

OTHER NOTES

The Metropolitan Police wishes Mr Shipman and Ms West all the best for their upcoming nuptials.

COMPLETED BY: P.C. PLOD

OFFICER NUMBER: PSO24987482

Nessa's

Essential Facts

Life can be a cruel mistress, I know. It's not easy bein' me and it's probably harder bein' you. I've had some good times, I've had some bad times; I've had my ups and my downs; I've been through the mill and I've done whatever the opposite is. There's a lotta wisdom in this brain of mine (too much for the back of a postage stamp, as it turns out – so I had to scrap that idea) and I want to share that wisdom with you now. The instruction manual for life got lost in the loft long, long ago – so here's my very own top five essential facts for living. They've helped me through the years and I'd be surprized if they don't help you.

1) Love isn't blind, it's just invisible. You've no idea when it's going to arrive or what direction it'll come from. And like a dose of the clap, once it's arrived it's hell to shift. All you can do is get on with your life and wait for it to attack. As my commanding officer in the Marines once said, 'Expect the unexpected'. He unfortunately died shortly after telling me that – but those mines were hard to spot.

2) Know who your friends are and stand by them no matter what. When you need a helping hand, when you're in your hour of need, everyone should have a friend to turn to. A good friend is the most valuable thing in the world. Well, technically, certain drugs are more valuable – and they're easier to smuggle across certain borders – but I'm not going through all that again. I'm not going back to that jail for no one. End of.

3) Good things come to those who wait, but only the good die young. All I'm saying is: if you're going to wait for something good, do it somewhere safe, see?

4) Making money on the stock market is a piece of cake. Losing money on the stock market is considerably easier, so unless you're Albert Einstein I'd leave it well alone. I dabble every once in a while and, I won't lie to you, I even got so far as setting up my own relative value hedge fund using asset-backed securities and relative volatility arbitrage. But I'm sure you can see the gaping hole in that idea and thank God I did too before it was too late. Save your money for the slots.

5) Above all, always be yourself – that's all anyone can ask. Well, if you're a prisoner of war, you can also be asked for your name, rank, date of birth and serial number. I wish I'd known that back in Belize. But, normally, people will only ask you to be yourself.

VANESSA SHANESSA JENKINS

PROFILE:

Alrigh'. I'm Nessa. I'm dead easy to get on with. I don't take crap from nobody. I gets the job done. And that's about all you need to know about me personally. I've done far too many jobs to note down, so what follows is just a brief overview. If you would like the full list then send a very large, stamped, addressed jiffy bag to me and I'll sort you out with one. Okay?

CAREER HISTORY:

The Slots, Amusement Administrator (Current)

I currently hold a senior position at a well-known recreation centre in Barry. My job includes stopping people when they've put too much money in the slot machines then testing them to see if they are ever going to pay out, and shouting 'Oi!' at any kids who try and rock the 10p machine.

The Dolphin, Publican (2004)

As well as bartending, my job included propping up Maurice after he fell off his stool, booting out tramps, not selling cigarettes to the local primary school kids and informing any foreigners that it's not safe to stay in there for too long. That Scott Mills from Radio 1 was there in the summer. He was riskin' it.

Jail, Inmate (Undisclosed)

The less said about this the better. I regret it. I won't be doing it again. But I made the best out of a bad situation – it's a skill I have. While I was incarcerated I made friends and did a lot of networking. Now I'm welcome in over 200 illegal gambling dens in the UK. I can find the positive in every situation.

Eddie Stobarts (2002)

I spent many a happy day in the belly of a 'Scania R Series' driving up and down the country. There really is something beautiful about looking out over the virgin, untouched forests, hills and valleys of Great Britain from the cab of your twelve-tonne, toxic-chemical truck. During that time I developed a great patience with the roads of this country, making me a more balanced and centred human being.

he Street, Street Performer (1998)

I can be very still when I want to be, thanks to an extensive meditation course I took back in the 80s. So I thought I'd take these talents to the public and perform as a human statue. To be honest, I still occasionally work as Charlie Chaplin for a little extra cash on the side. Although these days I earn much more than I did then – but that's inflation for you.

The Who World Tour, Driver (1996)

Most of the time I spent driving the boys around, but occasionally I took over and did a bit of tour-managing. I had a very enjoyable time with Roger and the lads. But when push comes to shove, I didn't like Townsend one bit. He spent far too much time on his computer researching and not enough time practising. And at the end of the tour there was no book. All that research wasted.

All Saints, Singer/Manager (1993)

Fun times. Majority of my time was spent in the studio, but occasionally I did get involved in the more managerial side of things. They originally wanted to be called Hawthorne Avenue, named after the street where Melanie lived. I said 'no way, why don't we call ourselves after the road that this studio's on'. They did and 'All Saints' were born.

BBC, News Producer (1986)

The woman behind Kate Adie – that's who I was. For ages she was going on about 'Oh – can we do a story on this car boot sale?' or 'I've got this article I want to do about a waterskiing canary.' But I put my foot down and said 'If you want to get anywhere in television then you have to get out there and report from major war zones. You need to put yourself at risk. Then you'll gain the respect of your fellow reporters and the Great British public.' She was reluctant at first, but then took to it like a duck to water. We saw some horrors in our time, but Kate always kept her sense of humour – so we'd always laugh it off in the hotel bar afterwards.

Navy Officer (1982)

Classified. That's all I'm gonna say.

REFEREES:

EDDIE STOBART (CEO)
Eddie Stobarts
Stobart Towers
Cumbria
UK

DAVE (CEO/Manager/Driver)
Dave's Coaches
Barry Island
Wales

NESSA'S

Guide to Trucking

As you have probably worked out, I am no longer employed here at Eddie Stobarts. Now that's partly because I fell out of love with the open road and partly because I fell out with Eddie. He's a top bloke, but if it's love you're after ... you'll only end up getting hurt. I reckon he's a player. And when you own a fleet of trucks as large as he does, I guess that's your right.

Anyways. Welcome to your new job. It's not going to be pleasant – but then again what job is? I've learned a lot from the highways of this great country, so thought I would pass that knowledge on to my successor. That's you, by the way.

I'll give it to you straight – driving trucks is boring. There's a lot of road out there and it's all pretty much the same (except for the M6 toll, which is a pleasure to drive on – but at £9 a go, it does eat into your per diems) so you will find yourself getting bored pretty quickly. When this happens, I like to turn on the radio. But, to be honest, Radio 1's not as exciting since Chris Evans left, I don't really like Jonathan Ross which rules Radio 2 out, I can't for the life of me get Radio 3 in that cab, and Radio 4 is full of predictable plays which always end with someone dying or getting a terminal illness or something – it's not very happy and it doesn't pass the time. So here's

another tip: if you've got the money, I can recommend hiring a 'trucker's mate'. They have to listen to what you say and agree with you and then, once you've run out of conversation, they have to entertain you. Don't get two trucker's mates, though. I tried that. They just talk to each other and pretty much ignore you the whole journey. I haven't tried three trucker's mates – could improve the situation. Might be worth a try. Who knows?

Quite often, you will see reminders telling you that tiredness kills and that you should take a break. While this is a conspiracy by the companies that own the service stations, it's no secret your seven-and-a-half-tonne truck is best piloted with your eyes open. It can be done with 'em shut, but not for long and it's not for the faint-hearted. If you're feeling knackered, I can recommend dissolving a couple of ProPlus in a can of Red Python. Not easy to get in this country anymore, Red Python, due to its illegally-high levels of guarana, but you can order it by the crate from the internet. That definitely keeps you going. On your drive you might well see signs saying 'This sign is not in use', when it clearly is.

Now this is very important, so keep reading, okay? To communicate with the other truckers you'll be using your CB radio. There are two very important rules. Number one: always end your communication with the word 'over'. If you don't use it, you'll end up with very long and awkward silences. Number two: you need to pick a good handle. The best ones are taken, so don't be thinking you can use your full name and don't go for anything like 'Trucker', 'Eddie Stobart' or 'Dr Haulage' because, trust me, they'll all be in use. It's best to go for the sort of names most truckers wouldn't think of – names like 'Peter Ustinov', 'The Charioteer' or 'Logistic Barbera' are all much better choices.

Here's another tip, and I'm not going to tell you this twice – only ever use the air horn when you're on the road. With a power of 135 decibels it'll badly damage a pedestrian's ears. Eddie once told me the story of a man whose head exploded because he was stood next to an air horn – although don't take what Eddie says literally 'cos he does like to exaggerate. But it gets the point across. Most importantly, NEVER use it between the hours of 11pm and 7am. It's inconsiderate and against the law. The horn is your friend – treat it well and the road is yours.

Finally, it's best not to wear a skirt when trucking – the cab is high up off the ground and it's not uncommon to need a bunk-up. For this reason, never go to work 'commando'. When Scotty was wearing his kilt that fateful St Andrew's day, the boys at the depot got quite an eyeful and some of the names they gave him afterwards were very hurtful.

That's it! All I can say now is good luck.

Seriously, you'll need it.

ROAD TRIP GUIDE

From Barry
to Billericay

As I'm much too old to have a 'Gap Year' now, I fear that I'll never get round to writing a travel guide for some far off exotic place. However, while it's not exactly Thailand, there are still many sights of wonder on the journey I am now making every couple of months. Barry to Billericay. So in case you might be making a journey from South Wales to Essex, I thought I could share with you some of the UK's best kept secrets. Obviously if you're travelling the other way, from Essex to South Wales, then read this from the bottom up else you'll miss all but one of them.

CARDIFF

Well, I say 'Cardiff' but obviously that's not a very specific attraction, is it? You can't just stop off and look at an entire city, can you? (Unless you're on a hill, in which case you can. Thought these days there might be a pylon in the way – or some mist) But there's a reason I'm being particularly vague. And that's because I don't know which bit I'm actually referring to. The thing is, and you probably won't believe me when I tell you this, but many scenes from the television series Dr Who are filmed in Cardiff! Yes! Cardiff! How do they make it look so futuris-

tic, I hear you ask? Well, it's probably with special effects. Anyway, my advice is have a little drive through Cardiff on your way, just in case you're lucky enough to catch a glimpse of David Tennant, Billie or maybe even an actual live Cyberman! If you don't know what Dr Who is though, I'd give this a miss.

IKEA BRISTOL

You've barely set foot in England before it's time for another stop off. This time at a place which will blow your mind with furniture. Ikea. If, like me, you thought you'd seen every kind of furniture there is to see, think again, buster! A couple of tips if you go there. Firstly, take a little pencil and a paper tape measure at the entrance, whether you're buying or not. They are free gifts so you are perfectly entitled to take them away, no purchase necessary. I clarified this with an Ikea employee to avoid unwittingly participating in any illegal activity. Half way round, stop off at the cafe and sample some genuine Swedish meatballs. If I'm honest, they kind of taste the same as normal meatballs, so perhaps it's the

2

atmosphere that makes them feel more Swedishy. Finally, as the shop is so large, fatigue will set in by the time you reach the rugs. This can lead to arguments. I got quite shirty with Gwen last time, but you just have to remind yourself that this behaviour is perfectly understandable in these circumstances so you have to try and bite your tongue.

THAMES VALLEY PARK, READING ✈

Computer folk have called Reading the UK's answer to 'Silicon Valley'. Accolades surely don't get any higher than that, do they? All your technology biggies are in this business park, like Microsoft and all of the other ones. I like to take a little detour through Thames Valley Park and see which companies I recognise. You'll often hear me say 'Ooh! They made my colour jet printer!', 'Look! That company made some software I use for editing digital photographs,' or 'That's Microsoft, there.' The only way I can describe a visit to Thames Valley Park is that it feels like you're at the centre of the universe. A hundred years from now, this place will be one of the UK's most prized historical attractions, you mark my words!

IKEA WEMBLEY 🍽 ✈

The main reason I'm putting this one in, is that sometimes I see an item of furniture in Bristol Ikea and I spend the whole of the M4 wishing I'd bought it. Once it was a fold-down computer desk. Unbelievable bargain, £30. Another time it was a very neat £15 set of occasional tables. However, if this happens, you can simply nip off the M25 to Ikea in Wembley. It'll add an hour/hour and

a half to your journey (depending on whether you have some more meatballs or not) but better a short delay than a lifetime of regret.

SOUTH MIMMS SERVICES 🍽 ✈

Quite simply, these are top-quality services. Get this; retail outlet, three fast food restaurants, picnic area, children's playground, cash machine, arcade. Pretty good, huh? But buckle up, sunshine, 'cos it doesn't end there; petrol station, gents, ladies, disabled toilet, baby-changing facilities. Still want more? Well then, I'd consider you greedy and you'll probably need to find another services because that's everything that South Mimms has to offer. I can highly recommend a special type of sandwich which they import from Italy called a 'panini'. The best way I can describe it is, it's basically a toastie, but with a continental twist – French bread. Imagine that!

CHELMSFORD 🍽 ✈

A bit of a detour from Billericay this, but if time is on your side, pop over there and look at the sign as you enter Chelmsford. It tells you that Chelmsford is 'England's Oldest Settlement'.

3

Amazing. If I'm honest though, that sign's the most exciting part of Chelmsford, so once you've seen it you might as well head back to Billericay.

YOU'VE NOW REACHED BILLERICAY!

So, our odyssey has come to an end after a thoroughly enjoyable 3 hours 41 minutes on the road, according to my Route Master

software (not including stops). I should point out that the Sat Nav says it should be 3 hours 48. Don't ask me where that discrepancy comes from. Rest assured, I shall be emailing Route Master to find out.

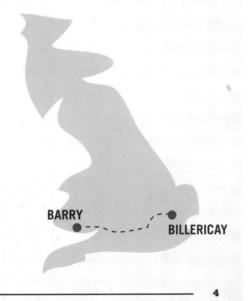

BARRY

BILLERICAY

4

bebo

Home **Browse** **Find People** **Forums** **Music** **More**

Search

Bryn is in your extended network (and family)

View My: Pics Videos

Contacting Bryn

⊗ Send Message

☝ Forward to friend

 Rank user

👤+ Add to friends

👉 Add to favourites

⊗ Block user

BRYN'S INTERESTS

'My name means hill in Welsh!'

Male
42 Years Old
Barry, Wales

Last login: *3mins ago*

BRYN'S DETAILS

Status:	Single
Here For:	Networking, Friends
Hometown:	Barry, Wales
Ethnicity:	White Welsh
Religion:	80% Christian, 20% Buddhist
Children:	None that I know of! But seriously, none.

Bryn's Latest Blog Entry

Dear blog reader,

Welcome to another exciting instalment of Bryn's blog. So, 'What has Bryn been up to?' I hear you ask. Well, it's been a busy 24 hours

buddy). Driving with satellite navigation technology, updating my myspace page.

thing that happened. Imagine, being able to watch Sky in the bedroom too! It's like being in the royal family. Another thing that happened was I googled' my name and found out that there's a basketball player who plays for Columbia West University in America called 'Bryn West' too. Small world, eh? What's more, this lad is 6'8'. What a strapping young fellow he must be. That's about it for now. Log on tomorrow for my next update.

Yours sincerely,

Bryn

▲ View all 360 blogs

Bryn has **14** Friends

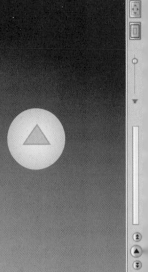

Watch 'Musical Tribute
to Heath Ledger' again...

MUSIC

James Blunt, Jack Johnson, Damian Rice, Norah Jones, Fatboy Slim, Tom Jones, Katherine Jenkins, McFly, Billy Joel, R Kelly (Ballads only), Bryan McFadden (solo material only). Brian May (solo material only), Beverley Craven, Paul McCartney (solo material only)

FILMS

To be honest, I've yet to see a film I didn't like. They're all so well done, aren't they? But absolute favourites include: Brokeback Mountain, The Matrix Trilogy and the Truman Show (makes you think, doesn't it? Is this world real? Or is it just a big television show?). My Own Private Idaho.

TELEVISION

The Gadget Show (it's a show all about the latest gadgets). My Hero (what a concept! Get this, its about a Superhero living in suburbia. He has a talking baby too! Where do they get their ideas from?). The News (not fussy which channel, but it's always good to keep up with current events. And its better than any drama show 'cos you never know what will happen next). The Weather (I just find it useful rather than entertaining).

BOOKS

I'm not into novels as such, but I am a regular in the 'Humour' section of Waterstones. Favourites are Crap Towns, The World According To Clarkson (the man's hilarious!). The QI Annual (great for pub discussions). And Another Thing: The World According To Clarkson 2 (where does he get his hilarious opinions from?). The World Of Karl Pilkington (if you think Ricky Gervais is funny, you should check out this guy!). Round Ireland With A Fridge (the fella only went and did it for a bet! I ask you!)

HEROES

Malcolm X, Martin Luther King, Nelson Mandela, my brother Trevor West. All of them did wonderful work for civil rights in the 20th Century (not including Trevor).

Doris <Deadlydoris82>

ONLINE NOW

Doris
What's wrong with a cheeky finger?

Gender:
Female

Last Active
Online Now!

Member Since
3rd Feb 2005

Share the Luv
77

Music
biffy clyro, crystal castles, daft punk, jamie t, kanye west, dirty pretty things, klaxons, hundred reasons, the killers, linkin park, editors, the fratellis, kasabian, foals, guillemots, lethal bizzle, arcade fire, babyshambles, hard-fi, 30 seconds to mars, hot chip, the kooks, the libertines.

Scared Of:
b in put in a old pplz h0me. dem hudies player h8ing me wen i wlk down alleys. dodg boylar n wintR. carbN m0n0xide poyznin.

Happiest When:
ww2 ended. i h8ed rati0ning. i h8ed blakouts. waz totally the shizzle. ded happy wen it waz all don n dust3d. also luv clubn. speshly wiv me m8s. wkd tyms.

To All My Haters:
you got luv 4 me, i got luv 4 u. so dont go h8ing on me or me sistaz. coz we aint h8ing u.

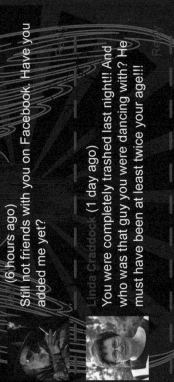

(6 hours ago)
Still not friends with you on Facebook. Have you added me yet?

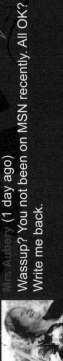

Linda Craddock (1 day ago)
You were completely trashed last night!! And who was that guy you were dancing with? He must have been at least twice your age!!!

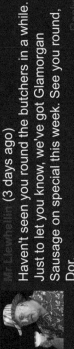

Mrs Aubery (1 day ago)
Wassup? You not been on MSN recently. All OK? Write me back.

Mr Llewhellin (3 days ago)
Haven't seen you round the butchers in a while. Just to let you know, we've got Glamorgan Sausage on special this week. See you round, Dor.

Mrs Walters (4 days ago)
I PM'd the government about the paving slab that's come loose on the high street. So you don't have to. I'll message you when I hear anything.

Ted (5 days ago)
You look well hot in your photo. Look Dor, I've tried adding you on Facebook but it doesn't

Mr Phillips   Linda Craddock   Maude & Dewi   Mrs Walters   Ted   Mrs Aubery   Mr Llewhellin   Rhodri Thomas

Polls

GRUNGE

Click on a Poll to see results

Do you need a stair-lift yet? (13 Votes)

Who's your favourite Beverley Sister? (4 Votes)

Are you still allowed to drive? (15 Votes)

Have your children put you in a home yet? (14 Votes)

False or real teeth? (22 Votes)

Do you think I'm sexy? (18 Votes)

Who's going to pop their clogs next? (4 Votes)

Photo Albums

GRUNGE

Doris'

Dating Tips for: Girls / Homos

1 Don't go sellin' him the whole farm on the first date. Obviously you can let him have a kiss, a cuddle. And maybe, if he behaves himself, a cheeky finger. It worked for me back in the forties and it still works now, I can tell you.

2 Body language is key. Copy the fella's movements. This'll make him feel comfortable with you. (Obviously don't copy them exactly else you'll look like a right idiot.) And keep wetting your lips. He'll be gagging for it.

3 By all means show a bit of boob. Or you could wear a short skirt. But for the love of Jesus don't do both. You want him to see you as a slut – not as a cheap prostitute.

4 Never underestimate the power of the ganja. A quick toke before your night out and your dating worries will quickly fade. Make sure it's good shit, mind. Fellas don't like a gibbering paranoid wreck.

'Thing to remember is – don't go giving him nothing on the first night ... a kiss, a cuddle, a cheeky finger – just don't go selling him the whole farm.' Doris

Dating Tips for: Boys / Dykes

1 To catch yourself a bit of skirt who's way out of your league – try 'negging'. The super hotties are used to young fellas fawning over them all the time, so build up her confidence then use a negative comment to knock her down a peg or two. After this she'll notice you and will want your approval. For example: 'Nice cardigan. My grandma has one very similiar to that.' And abracadabra! You might be up for some action!

2 Get blotto. It's more common for a fella to use phrases like 'I love you' and 'You're amazing' when they're trolleyed. Us birds love that sort of thing. Plus it'll give you the confidence to approach them – if you're really frazzled you might even find that you've asked them to marry you. But don't worry, divorce was invented for a reason.

3 Always ask her questions. She won't want to know about you, you're probably boring, so ask about her. To be fair, she won't be much more interesting, but if you appear to be a good listener then she's more likely to give you 'special time' later on.

4 Pay your way. If you want to be a player then you have to show everyone how big your manhood is. The best way to do that is to appear to have lots of money. So buy everything for her, that way she'll be under the impression that you are rich and have a massive man spanner. Quids in!

Smithy and ~~Gavlar's~~
Mainly Smithy's

BEERS
of the WORLD

ie ~~"Best Ever Beers"~~
Beers Bonanza

ESSEX
Aescwine Mild
Essex is the centre of the beeriverse and this is the best tipple of them all. Brewed down the road at Basildons oldest brewery, it's known to its friends as 'Arse'. Equally good for a lunchtime loosener as it is for a silly weekend session. Has magical properties beyond the ten-pint mark.
Rated: 10 pints

MEXICO
El Peligroso
El beer! Tastes like grout and contains some sort of herb that's only legal in Cancun. Blinding. Quite literally.
Rated: 75 pints

THAT BIT
Very hard to get beer from here. Smithy reckons they haven't invented it yet and plans one day to become a beer missionary.

USA – Ulysses S. Grant's Union Stout
This beers-arse is an all-American action hero. Weirdly fizzy and Gav reckons it's made with urad or something (which is clearly bullshit because I've tried putting urad in my home-brew and it comes out horrible). Still, it's always on two-for-one down the offie so it'd be rude not to. Goes very well with a full English.
Rated: 8 pints

FRANCE – Femme
Batteur (aka Wife Beater)
What else? It's fighting fuel of the highest grade. Not really my cup of tea, but then it isn't anyone's cup of tea because that would be tea and this is lager. Gavlar loves it though.
Rated: 7 pints

FINLAND Leikki Olut
Smithy found this one tucked right at the back of a shelf in the corner shop, so we're not sure they make it any more. Or if its actually a beer. And we're not sure it's Finnish, but the label does feature a herring. Thankfully, though it doesn't taste of fish just beer. Really, really good beer.
Rated: 8.5 pints

GERMANY
Jahrennes Nase Bier
This is a little beauty! It's
fermented for nine years in the
North Rhine-Westphalia region
(wherever that is). De-bloody
beautiful. Goes
well with crisps and gives a
mellow hangover.
Rated: 8.5 pints

RUSSIA – Something that looks like 'tommbo parketbl'
You'd struggle to read the label before you even start,
let alone after a few of these Russki wrist wrestlers.
But it's a good-looking bottle and the taste doesn't let you
down. Best drunk cold on a warm, summer's evening
whilst watching a porno.
Rated: 7 pints

SPAIN – Tres Hesmanos
Ooh yes. A ripper. This one's
sweeter than Gavlar's face when
he's sleeping but has more wallop
than Lucy when she's in a mood.
Expensive, but worth every
penny. Delicious.
Rated: 9 pints

JAPAN = Armstrong Ale
The Japs know a thing or two
about beer it would seem 'cos
this one's a contender for the top
spot! Comes in massive bottles
which gets you pissed much
quicker, but it goes down beauti-
fully and smells of bananas. Just
don't let it get warm.
Rated: 9.5 pints

AUSTRALIA – Eagle Bitter
Smithy doesn't like this one at all, but I
think it's lovely. Really tasty and rich.
I've got an Ozzie mate at work who's
never heard of it but according to the
packaging this beer's won silver prize
at the Global Beerfest for the last six years
running. Love to go one day, but Global
Beerfest doesn't show up on Google.
Rated: 6.5 pints

little hoppy with great head

Armstrong Ale

EAGLE BITTER

Smithy's

Home-Brew Instructions...

The nectar of life!
Beautiful, cheap, lovely bees
in just A0 A1 A2 A3 A4
15 steps!

STEP -1
Sterilize EVERYTHING with sachets from Boots. Wish I'd realized this earlier.

STEP 0
Put the kettle on and wash hands.

STEP 0.5
WASH 'EM AGAIN!

STEP 1
Chuck all the ingredients in the plastic tub thing (THE ONE WITHOUT A TAP ON THE FRONT): the gloop from the 'Best Bitter' pack, one-and-a-half kettles' worth of boiling water, 6 packs of icing castor brown plain sugar and 33 pints of tap water. Stir it up and leave it till it's only just warm.

STEP 2
Put in the little granules (yeast?) from the yellow sachet. DON'T USE A STERILISING SACHET – IT'S DIFFERENT STUFF. Learnt that the hard way.

STEP 3
Put the lid on.

STEP 4
Put it in the airing cupboard next to the hot water tank.

STEP 4.25
Don't let it drip on Rudi's hoodies. She might tip it down the lav.

STEP 4.5

MAKE SURE THERE'S WATER IN THE LITTLE WIGGLY PIPE STICKING OUT THE TOP OF THE TUB. Made that mistake once and it all went vinegary. TASTED LOVELY ON CHIPS THOUGH.

STEP 5

Come back in a week to see if it's stopped fizzing. If it hasn't, go to step 4. If it's exploded, wash all the towels in the airing cupboard, blame the hot water tank's dodgy TPR valve and go back to step -1.

STEP 6

Use a bit of hose to suck the stuff out into the plastic keg (THE ONE WITH A TAP ON THE FRONT). DON'T blow bubbles. DON'T touch the sticky goo at the bottom. DON'T drink it yet (note to self: remember New Year's Eve '05 and the bathroom clean-up cost).

STEP 7

ADD THE SMITHSTER'S SECRET INGREDIENT!!! NO ONE MUST KNOW! Keep it secret. Plus: a dollop of Marmite and as much sugar as fits on a beermat + a raw potato (SMALL) + curry powder + can of cider + pickled egg + fish finger + toothpaste + coffee + tea bag + rosemary & garlic IF IT AIN'T BROKE, SMITHSTER!! + corn on the cob?

STEP 8

Screw the lid on TIGHT! (Use rubber gloves.) Put back in the airing cupboard next to the hot water tank for two days and pray to the god of beer.

STEP 9

If it explodes, reassure the neighbours it wasn't a bomb and go back to step -1. Otherwise, move the keg to the shed for two weeks.

STEP 10

Test a bit on Rudi's nail varnish: if it comes off with a wipe, the beer's ready. If it just smudges, give it another week in the shed + some more sugar

STEP 10A

Get battered!

Simple as that! ~~33~~ ~~45~~ ~~33~~
15 Pints of loveliness for just
~~£35~~ ~~£67~~ ~~£145~~
£145

Dear Ness,

Hello stranger! Now I know that I'm probably not top of the old 'pen pal' list right now (or 'Friends Reunited' - or whatever you kids are in to), but I couldn't let things just finish the way they did. Fair play, you've had a think about how things are going with us, the relationship, the 'affair' and you've made a decision to 'cool' things between us. And you're quite entitled to do that.

But come on, you must admit we've got a lot going for us, haven't we? There must be a bit of you that still wants a piece of the Madeley, no? I also think you haven't considered the consequences of finishing with me. Here's an example: even after we've split, I'm concerned that you'll just go around comparing every man to me. And that's not fair on them or you, because realistically none of them will match up to me. Where else will you find a suave, articulate, erudite, worldly and well-groomed man like me? I'll tell you where: nowhere, that's where. I suppose what I'm trying to say is that if it's not me you want, then perhaps men aren't for you after all.

However, if you ultimately do decide that there's no way back for us, then there is something rather serious I should raise with you. The VHS Cassette tape we made. I'll be needing that back (the original please, not a copy. It was a TDK 240 min tape, so don't think I won't notice). To be quite honest, that tape could do some serious damage to my marriage, or even worse, my TV career. I'm seen as a wholesome family man and if the tabloids got hold of it then I fear the public may react very badly to some of the 'post-watershed' activities we took part in. I will get my P.A. to include a stamped, addressed jiffy bag for you just in case.

Yours sincerely,

Anonymous

Ps.
My P.A. has probably also enclosed a signed photo, as she does with all outgoing mail. If you don't want it, please give it to a fan you know or simply send it back in the jiffy bag.

SMITHY'S BEST EVER ENGLAND XI

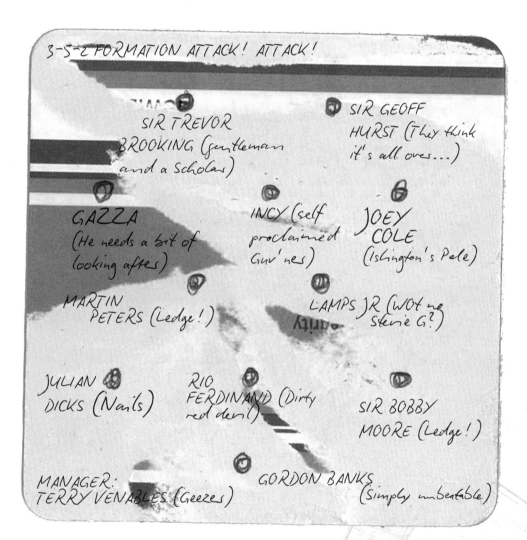

3-5-2 FORMATION ATTACK! ATTACK!

SIR TREVOR BROOKING (gentleman and a Scholar)

SIR GEOFF HURST (they think it's all over...)

GAZZA (He needs a bit of looking after)

INCY (self proclaimed Guv'ner)

JOEY COLE (Islington's Pele)

MARTIN PETERS (Ledge!)

LAMPS JR (WOt no Stevie G?)

JULIAN DICKS (Nails)

RIO FERDINAND (Dirty red devil)

SIR BOBBY MOORE (Ledge!)

MANAGER: TERRY VENABLES (Geezer)

GORDON BANKS (Simply unbeatable)

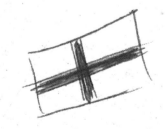

facebook

home   account   privacy   logout

Profile edit   **Friends** | ▼   **Inbox** ▼

Search

Applications edit

🖼 Photos
👥 Applications
📋 Marketplace
📅 Events
≫ Superprod!
🖼 Likeness
➤ Friends GPS

Share you photos with friends on Facebook

Neil Smith

is still drunk from three days ago.

Updated on Monday edit

Network:	Essex
Sex:	Oi Oi!
Relationship status	It's extremely complicated
Hometown:	Billericay

▼ **Information**

Interests: West Ham Utd. Mates. Family. Work. Pub. Beer. Quizzes. Having a Laugh. Pleasure.

Favourite Music: Dance Mix '99. Bangin' Tunez '99. House Anthems '99. Floorfillaz '99. Sound Assembly '99. 99's Massive Choons. Dance Boom '99. Hyper Party '99. Now That's What I Call Music 1999.

Favourite TV Shows: Anything on Nuts TV or Bravo. Eurotrash. Ten minute porn preview. How To Look Good Naked.

Favourite Movies: Basic Instinct. Wild Things. Emmanuelle. Showgirls. Boogie Nights. Top Gun.

Favourite Books: What is this? School?!!

Favourite Quotes: 'I'm forever blowing bubbles' Bobby Moore Stand
'I'm forever blowing bubbles' Michael Jackson!!!!!
'It's the last thing you expect to find when you come into work in the morning' the legend that is Michael Shipman

▼ **Mini-Feed**

Displaying 4 stories   Import | See all

▼ **The Wall**

Displaying 5 of 104 wallposts   Import | See all

Write something on your own wall...

View photos of Neil (108)

View Neil's Friends (110)

Prod Neil

Drop-kick Neil

▼ **Friends**
87 friends   See all

Bryn   Budgie   Lucy
                              Radcliffe

▼ **Photos**
1 of 14 albums   See all

Lucy Radcliffe (Billericay) wrote at 4.52pm

Hello my Smithywithywoowoo
ru coming2watch me trampolining l8r?
btw, can't go laser quest wit u on s@urday. guides camping trip

Lulabellamozarella xoxoxoxoxo

West ham tribute

▼ **Groups**

4 groups   See all

Say It Loud, Essex & Proud • Join This Group If You Think Rudi Smith Is A Dickhead • Billericay Youth Theatre Production:Romeo & Juliet • Plumbers Make The Best Lovers • Stop The Phone Mast • I Love Ritzy's Foam Night

Pam Shipman (Billericay) wrote at 3.25pm on Jan 26, 2008

Coo-wee! Hello Smithy, it's Pam here! Funny meeting you on here! Seeing as Gavin doesn't seem to want to reply to my little messages, I thought I might give you a go. Also, have you got Stace's facebook address? Text it to me if you have.

PS. We're having Steak for tea tonight. I'll put an extra couple or three on if you want to pop round!

▼ **Gifts**

You have 4 gifts   Send a Gift

From Stacey

From Pam Shipman

From Gavin

Gavin Shipman (Billericay) wrote at 11.14am Jan 25, 2008

Smithy, why did you put that picture of me at the foam night in 2002 on facebook for, you twat? People have seen it at work now. Some of them keep giggling when I walk past.

Bryn West (Barry) wrote at 11.14am Jan 25, 2008

Hiya Smithy! Just thought I'd let you know, I did 100 press ups this morning! I could never have done that before I got the gym. You should come over and have another session with me soon. Right, must go. I have some more facebook buddies to tell about my feat!

Chinese Alan (Billericay) wrote at 4.16pm Jan 14, 2008

I'd have to say...

Cruise - Jodie Foster. If the ship got hijacked, she'd sort it out no worries.
Marry - KD Lang. Nice voice. Would win karaoke every week with her.
Shag - Martina Navratilova. Think about her stamina levels...

Okay, here's one back Moira Stuart, Angela Rippon, Jan Leeming...

Karl 'Budgie' Barrett (Billericay) wrote at 1.11pm Jan 8, 2008

Just thought I'd send you a message to say you're a bender

Bryn's

Film Recommendations

BROKEBACK MOUNTAIN 👍👍👍👍👍👍👍👍👍👍 **10 thumbs up!**

I do love a cowboy movie, but there is a twist to this movie which might surprize you. The cowboys are gay. That's right. Gay cowboys! I've never seen anything like it! And neither, I bet, have the likes of Clint Eastwood or Butch Cassidy. To make it worse, one of the gay cowboys is married. What a pickle! But, no, I loved the film. It was very well acted and the story was beautiful. I was, however, disappointed by the lack of Indians. Just one little shoot out in a corral would have made this film a little more exciting. Who knows, maybe the sequel will have some gay Indians in it. If you do get the chance to see this then I definitely would. If for no other reason than to see two gay cowboys! What will they think of next? Gay astronauts?

2001: A SPACE ODYSSEY 👍👍👍👍👍👍👍👍👍

I admit that this film is now historically inaccurate. Back in 2001 I didn't even have a USB memory stick, let alone a spaceship! It's best to, in your mind at least, add about 40 years to the title – that way it makes it more believable. But I put this in here because it's worth seeing for all the gadgets that we might have in the future! There's a rather snazzy talking computer in it called HAL. But the future's not too far off! Dick Powell has this thing on his computer that you can talk to and it talks back! What it says doesn't make a lot of sense mind, and you do have to keep repeating yourself, but that's not the point. One day, rather than texting someone, you might be able to speak ➤

your message in to your phone, and have that turned in to a text message! Then your pal could get that message read back to him using the computer on his phone! Let me warn you – it is quite boring in a lot of places – so make sure you watch it with a friend so you can chat during the docking scenes. You'd have thought they'd have figured a quicker way to dock spaceships, wouldn't you?

SIXTH SENSE 👍👍👍👍👍👍👍👍👍👍 10 thumbs up!

In this film Bruce Willis plays a ghost who can only be seen by this 9-year-old boy. But there's a very novel twist to the story that makes it all the more exciting. It turns out that Bruce Willis … didn't know he was a ghost! He thinks he's a real man! Something I definitely didn't see coming. The film is full of ghoolies and ghosties, so it's best not to watch it at night and don't watch it anywhere where you might have to walk home on your own, as you will be frightened. That said, it's a great film, and the boy in it, even though he's only 9 years old, is very good at remembering his lines.

WATERSHIP DOWN 👍👍👍👍👍👍👍👍👍👍 10 thumbs up!

This film initially confused me. And I'll tell you for why. It's animated but it has blood in it. Now you don't get that in Shrek now, do you? And yet it does have a wonderful song in it about a rabbit with bright eyes which Gwen used to play all the time. I can't remember the name of the song exactly, but I think it was something like 'Ghost Rabbit'. However, don't let this confusion put you off, because the film itself is very beautiful. It also makes a very valid point – don't let any area get too over crowded. It's very sad to see those bunnies crushed to death, but it does deliver a very important health and safety message to the children who watch it: capacity warnings exist for a reason!

THE CRYING GAME 👍👍👍👍👍👍👍👍👍👍 10 thumbs up!

This start of the film is about the IRA but it quickly changes to something altogether different. There's a man who falls in love with a lady – but she's actually a man too! I found that bit very hard to get my head round at first, because for a while it didn't make sense: why would a man wear a dress? I had to really sit down and think hard about that. He's not an unattractive lady, mind. If he were an actual lady he'd be a corker. But he isn't. Other than that it's a very clever film with some very good actors in it. I particularly liked Miranda Richardson. Although she wasn't as funny as she was in Blackadder. It has all the classic elements – drama, action, confusion. Worth seeing because I can't believe quite how much the man looks like a woman. Also, you will be humming the theme tune all the way home. Or if you're watching it on DVD at home you might already be humming it.

Relationship Do's & Don'ts

1 Remember that the word 'obliged' is not in your dictionary. If she invites you out to see her friends and you don't want to go – then don't go! She chose to go out with you, so it's basically her fault if you choose to be awkward. She has to take you as she found you.

2 Once you're in a relationship give it ten to fifteen years before you consider getting married. That way you can be sure what you're getting into. You don't want to be too impulsive.

3 Don't let yourself fall in love. That's for weaker guys. If you let such things happen then she'll be the one who ends up wearing the trousers. Which logically means you, my friend, will be wearing the apron. By all means say the words 'I love you', but know that in your heart of hearts you're actually saying 'I love West Ham'.

4 Remember: keep your girlfriend close but your drinking friends closer. I can't stress how important this is. Who's going to pick you up when you're paralytic in the gents? Your friends. Your girlfriend'll just moan at you to drink less. Who's going to make sure you get home safely? Well it's not your girlfriend. She

can't, she was off home three hours ago 'cos her parents have set a 9pm curfew during the school term. And most importantly, who'll still be there when your girlfriend dumps you?

5 It's completely natural to own up to a dozen porno videos. So don't let her tell you any different. And it would be stupid to throw them out anyway 'cos if you split up that'll cost you a good £100 to replace them.

6 It's okay to cheat – but only if your girlfriend is cheating. Ideally it's best if neither of you twig that the other is sleeping with another person. So keep it to yourself, and hopefully she'll do the same, and that way you can keep going out with each other.

7 Make friends with her teachers. If you've never met her teachers before then you get a lot of odd stares when you wait for her outside the playground. Once they realize that you're a sound guy, then they don't seem as concerned … except for some Geography teachers who still threaten to call the police. Wanker.

8 If you do ever make the mistake of getting married then remember this: when you go on the holiday after the wedding, leave your phone switched on. You never know when a mate might try and ring you for the football results or just simply for a chat.

9 Don't make the mistake of going shopping with them. When girls talk about shopping they don't go in thinking 'I need to buy a t-shirt'. Ah no. You go from shop to shop hoping that she'll finally remember what she came in for – only to find that she didn't drag you in to town for anything in particular – wasting valuable FIFA 2008 time.

10 Everything's a test. If you don't want to waste your time getting shouted at, then just treat everything she says as a test. 'I forgot to bring my jacket' means 'Give me your jacket. I want to see how long you can stand in the cold.' When she says 'I don't know. What do you want to do?' that means 'I do know. But guess what I want to do.' And of course 'What are you thinking?' is code for 'Stop thinking about football.'

BRYN ON MICK

Who's the worst driver out of you two?

Well, I've only been in the car with him the once, and he's a sensible sort of chap. So I would have to say ... yes. Mick is probably a better driver.

What's their favourite TV program?

I think he might be a fan of the News after he starred on it not so long ago!! But seriously, he probably is a fan of the News, it is a very informative show.

What's their favourite song?

If he doesn't like James Blunt I'd be surprized – what's not to like? So I am going to go for "Wiseman" – because I do think that Mick is a wise man.

Who's got the best singing voice?

Cor blimey! You do ask some tough questions. I don't think I can make a call on that one. I do not know if Mick sings. So based on that information I will probably say me. But I will be happy to be proved differently at a Karaoke night.

What colour are his/her eyes?

I am terrible at noticing things like this. And I don't like to guess. But I'm guessing they're the same as Gavin's, which are a kind of hazel brown with an amber fleck.

What is their worst habit?

Mick is a lovely man. I do not believe he has any bad habits.

Who would win in a fight?

Mick is far too lovely to fight. I think we would sit down and have a nice cup of tea together and simply talk it through. The winner would be the one whose point made the most sense. A verbal fight, if you will. A war of words. A tussle of tongues. No. Just a quarrel.

What is their favourite drink?

Well he's a golfer. So I'm guessing he'd like a good old fashioned beer. And probably a fair few of them — I'd imagine. Not that I'm saying he's a drinker or that he has some kind of an alcohol problem. No sirree.

What is their favourite meal?

Mick's favourite meal? Let me think — Mick's favourite meal. Hmm, what would Mick like to eat? I think that Mick would like to eat anything that his lovely wife Pam had cooked for him.

Who's the funniest out of the two of you?

Well I don't like to boast, but I do know quite a lot of jokes. For example, what do you call a fish with no 'I's? Fsh. Although that doesn't work as well written down.

Which of you could drink the most?

Definitely Mick. I bet he has a fair few on the golf course. And after three Cinzano and lemonades I'm struggling.

What is their best feature?

He's got nice eyes, just like his son.

What is their worst feature?

His grey hair.

MICK ON BRYN

Who's the worst driver out of you two?

I do commute every day. So, without being unfair to Bryn, I think that suggests I'm better at driving.

What's their favourite TV program?

Bryn likes his comedy so I would say My Family. It's got something for everyone, that show.

What's their favourite song?

I think he'd be into something classy. Probably classical music.

Who's got the best singing voice?

It would have to be Bryn. I can't sing for toffee.

What colour are his/her eyes?

I'll have to ask Pam. She notices things like that.

What is their worst habit?

He does have a tendency to joke a little too much. Like spending all that money getting his 'My niece went to Greece and all I got was this lousy T-Shirt' shirt printed.

Who would win in a fight?

I'd win — there's not much to him.

What is their favourite drink?

Tea?

What is their favourite meal?

It better be omelettes — because that Gwen does love to make them.

Who's the funniest out of the two of you?

Now I've heard Bryn's jokes — and they don't get as good a laugh as the ones I tell down the golf club.

Which of you could drink the most?

He's a tiny fella, so I think I could probably drink more.

What is their best feature?

He's a very happy chap.

What is their worst feature?

I don't mean to be rude, but probably his jokes.

NESSA ON PAM

Who's the worst driver out of you two?

I'M NOT GONNA LIE TO YOU, IT'S PAM. SIMPLE AS. I'VE BEEN ON THE ROADS MAN AN' BOY (THO' I'VE NOT ALWAYS HAD A VEHICLE AT MY DISPOSAL). WHEREAS PAM'S A LATE STARTER. SO I BEEN TOLD.

What's their favourite TV program?

TO BE HONEST, I DON'T GET TO SEE MUCH TV THESE DAYS. SO I DON'T KNOW WHAT'S CURRENT. BUT I WOULD EXPECT HER TO LIKE LOVEJOY. NOT MY CUP OF TEA, IN ALL FAIRNESS, BUT I DO APPRECIATE THE ACTING TALENTS OF IAN MCSHANE.

What's their favourite song?

TRUTH BE TOLD I WOULDN'T KNOW. SOMETHING OF A DISCO NATURE I WOULD EXPECT, BUT DON'T QUOTE ME ON THAT.

Who's got the best singing voice?

I HAVE BEEN TOLD BY BOTH SIMON COWELL AND STOCK, AITKEN AND WATERMAN THAT MY VOICE IS OUTSTANDING - BUT IT'S JUST NOT SOMETHING I'M PARTICULARLY INTERESTED IN. TO ANSWER YOUR QUESTION: ME. I'M NOT BEIN' ARROGANT, THAT'S JUST THE WAY IT IS.

What colour are his/her eyes?

EASY. STEEL BLUE-GREY.

What is their worst habit?

IT'S NOT A HABIT, BUT IT'S HER VEGETARIANISM.
VEGETARIANS - I DON'T LIKE 'EM AND I DON'T
TRUST 'EM. NEVER HAVE. PAM'S GOOD AS GOLD, MIND.
SHE'S NOT LIKE YOUR TYPICAL VEGETARIAN.

Who would win in a fight?

YOU KNOWS THE ANSWER TO THAT ONE.

What is their favourite drink?

I VACILLATES BETWEEN THE TWO STOOLS ON
THIS. SHE'S EITHER A G & T OR A VODKA LIME.
DEFINITELY NOT A LAMBRINI GIRL THO'.

What is their favourite meal?

IT'S A TOSS UP BETWEEN QUORN OR TOFU. I'M GOING
TO GO WITH TOFU - NEVER DID CARE MUCH FOR QUORN.

Who's the funniest out of the two of you?

FUNNY 'QUEER' OR FUNNY 'HA-HA'?

Which of you could drink the most?

I DON'T WANT TO BE UNFAIR TO PAM, BUT I WOULD.
HANDS DOWN. THAT'S JUST THE WAY IT IS. AND I'D
BE HAPPY TO PROVE IT TOO - IF PROOF IS NEEDED.

What is their best feature?

SHE LIKES FENCING. ANY WOMAN WHO'S HANDY
WITH A BLADE IS ALRIGHT WITH ME.

What is their worst feature?

HER LOVE OF THE ROYAL FAMILY. IT GOES
AGAINST MY MARXIST VALUES.

PAM ON NESSA

Who's the worst driver out of you two?

I'm a lovely little driver as long as no one is watching. If I'm by myself I'm up there with Nigel Mansell. But if someone's watching me reverse into a parking space I go to pieces.

What's their favourite TV program?

Does she like Big Brother? I don't know if there is anyone out there who doesn't. I'm going to say Big Brother. Either that or Coast, 'cos she talks a lot about the sea.

What's their favourite song?

She likes trucks don't she? So it's probably a country song. '9 to 5' by Dolly Parton?

Who's got the best singing voice?

Probably Ness if I'm honest. She did such a wonderful performance at Gwen's surprise party. Definitely her. Unless I was singing alongside Mick, then I'd whip her.

What colour are his/her eyes?

I think the left one's blue and the right one's a bit browny.

What is their worst habit?

I'm not a superficial person - but she does use a little bit too much make-up. You'd never catch me doing that.

Who would win in a fight?

I don't want to blow my own trumpet - I am trained in a couple of forms of self defence. She's definitely stronger, although I know a couple of very powerful pressure points. And if I had a sword in my hand then she'd be in trouble, as Big Fat Sue can testify to.

What is their favourite drink?

I think she's a girl who knows her whiskey. All I know about whiskey is it tastes horrible – bring back Hooch, that's what I say.

What is their favourite meal?

She's travelled a bit so something a bit foreign and classy. Moussaka?

Who's the funniest out of the two of you?

I'd say me. Nessa seems like quite a solemn lady. When I'm on a night out with the girls you should hear some of the things we say. Although I try telling this stuff to Mick and he doesn't even crack a smile – but that's cos you have to be there when we say it.

Which of you could drink the most?

Ten years ago it would have been me. Definitely. But these days I fall over if I even smell alcohol.

What is their best feature?

Nessa's a very clever girl. She should go on Mastermind – she'd definitely win the million pounds.

What is their worst feature?

Probably the smoking. And her love of tattoos.

MR&MRS ™

SMITHY ON STACEY

Who's the worst driver out of you two?

Never seen her drive. But I'm guessin' she'd be the worst. 'Cos she's a girl. Tho' Lucy's a girl and she got 90% in her theory test, so I suppose you can't generalize.

What's their favourite TV programme?

Lost. Or Extreme Makeover. Or Hollyoaks omnibus.

What's their favourite song?

'It's Raining Men' or 'Son of a Preacher Man'?

Who's got the best singing voice?

Now this totally depends on what you're talking about. If we're talking about Ronan Keating and that guff – then probably her. But if you're talking about spitting out the riddims of 'World in Motion' by New Order then I'm your man.

What colour are his/her eyes?

Don't know. Don't care.

What is their worst habit?

She doesn't spend enough time without Gav. She needs to learn to let him have the day off on occasion and untie him from those apron strings.

Who would win in a fight?

I'd get pulverized by Gav if I attempted that ... plus I'm not going to punch a girl, am I? But I can beat up Rudi, dead easy. They're about the same size - so on paper I think I'd beat Stacey.

What is their favourite drink?

Some sort of cocktail with strawberries in.

What is their favourite meal?

Well she probably won't like KFC, McDonalds or Burger King, so I'm going to go with Nandos. She's a bit classy like that. Shops at River Island and everything.

Who's the funniest out of the two of you?

She's good fun for a girl, and she really makes me laugh so I think that probably ... I'm still the funniest. I'm yet to meet someone funnier than me. And I've met Jim Davidson.

Which of you could drink the most?

There's no need to even answer that question. But it's me.

What is their best feature?

She's fun and she makes my Gav happy.

What is their worst feature?

She doesn't speak proper Welsh. She just has the accent. And her voice is quite high, so I have no idea what she's saying in clubs. I just nod.

STACEY ON SMITHY

Who's the worst driver out of you two?

Oh god. Probably me. I'm terrible at it, I am. Keep getting the clutch and accelerator mixed up. It's gotten me into so much trouble that has.

What's their favourite TV programme?

The Football, obviously. I think he said he liked Stars in Their Eyes - or was that Nessa? Actually I think that was Nessa.

What's their favourite song?

Him and Gav do like to do the 'World in Motion' rap a lot. So I'd probably go for that.

Who's got the best singing voice?

Not me. I'm shocking. Although probably not Smithy either - he doesn't have what I would call a 'proper singing voice'. So I don't think either of us have a better voice. Pass.

What colour are his/her eyes?

Blue. Definitely blue.

What is their worst habit?

It's not a habit as much as a dance. His robot dance. Don't get me wrong, I like it. But he does it with Gav and Gav only. I don't feel like I can join in.

Who would win in a fight?

Smithy definitely would. I struggle to open a jar. If I kept up my Judith Chalmers boxercize I might stand a chance - but I doubt it.

What is their favourite drink?

It'll be beer of some sort. But I don't know which one - him and Gav have a list of their favourite beers. It's probably the one they read about in Nuts magazine.

What is their favourite meal?

I have seen him eat three steaks before. So perhaps steaks?

Who's the funniest out of the two of you?

Aw Smithy's very funny. It's definitely him. Although his jokes are sometimes a little too blue for my liking.

Which of you could drink the most?

Now this is a complex question. If we're talking about getting tipsy - I'd say Smithy. One glass of wine and I'm anyone's. But if we're talking 'flat on the floor drunk' I reckon it'd be me. After I'm tipsy I can just keep on going. Don't know why. Odd, isn't it? Don't tell Smithy I said that.

What is their best feature?

I think probably his best feature is his loyalty. He's a good friend to Gav.

What is their worst feature?

I think he should try spending less time with Gav. He needs to learn to untie those apron strings, tho' it's quite sweet really, how possessive he gets. Bless.

GAVIN ON GWEN

Who's the worst driver out of you two?

I don't think Gwen's ever driven a car in her life, so it's probably me. That said, put us both in the back seat when Bryn's at the wheel and I'm the worst by a long shot. Slow and steady's all very well, but not down the M4.

What's their favourite TV programme?

It's probably still Crimewatch, since Nessa apparently appeared on it several years ago. That sort of link is all she needs. She also likes Songs of Praise 'cos Dick Powell was on it once.

What's their favourite song?

Oh, I know this — it's that cover of 'Ghetto Superstar' — something about Ireland?

Who's got the best singing voice?

I can't sing, full stop. So it's Gwen.

What colour are his/her eyes?

Black in the middle and white around the edges. Can't remember what colour the bit in-between is though ...

What is their worst habit?

Phoning Stace right in the middle of when we're... you know... busy. She's got a sixth sense. Makes me feel weird just thinking about it.

Who would win in a fight?

I would never hurt a woman, so she'd win hands down. Especially if she came at me with her omelette pan...

What is their favourite drink?

Something with eggs in ... A snowball?

What is their favourite meal?

Omelette. No doubt.

Who's the funniest out of the two of you?

Stace says I'm pretty funny, but Gwen's accent makes me laugh. So let's call it a tie.

Which of you could drink the most?

I like a glass of wine every now and then as does Gwen. Budgie's sure he saw me down a bottle of Taboo on our first trip to Magaluf though, so if me and Gwen went head-to-head on Taboo then I'd have the edge.

What is their best feature?

Omelettes (when all you want is an omelette).

What is their worst feature?

Omelettes (when you're really not in the mood for an omelette).

GWEN ON GAVIN

Who's the worst driver out of you two?

Oh, it's me. I'm terrible at it. I've only driven once and it took Trevor two weeks to get the dents out.

What's their favourite TV programme?

He's very technical, so it's probably something from the internet. Maybe it's Youtube?

What's their favourite song?

I'm not really sure. He hums quite a lot but I've absolutely no idea if it's even music, let alone which tune it is.

Who's got the best singing voice?

Well I'm no Shirley Bassey, but I overheard Gavin once in the shower at Pam and Mick's and I really thought he'd slipped and hurt himself.

What colour are his/her eyes?

A lovely shade of grey. They remind me of Wales.

What is their worst habit?

He always seems to be hurrying Stace off the phone when I call - often out-of-breath.

Who would win in a fight?

Ooh! Well, I don't think I'd stand much of a chance against that muscular young man. Unless Bryn lent me his rape alarm. Then I'd be able to get some help and might have a chance.

What is their favourite drink?

He does like beer. I would be more specific than that but I've served up a variety of different brands now and he doesn't seem to show a preference.

What is their favourite meal?

Omelette. I'm sure of it. He's very complimentary.

Who's the funniest out of the two of you?

Trevor always said I didn't have a sense of humour, so I'm probably not the best one to judge.

Which of you could drink the most?

What a peculiar question. I think the most I've ever had in one sitting is four cups of tea, and I've only ever seen Gavin drink one beer at a time, though it was a pint, so I imagine it would be close.

What is their best feature?

He's kind and loving and he makes my Stacey happy — and that's all I could want.

What is their worst feature?

A prominent chin.

Bryn's

Top Ten: Things to Do Before You Die

Now I'm not a morbid man – far from it – but there is a moment that comes to us all when you ask yourself, 'Have I lived life to the full? Have I experienced all that God's green Earth has to offer?' And unless you're Enrique Iglesias, I very much doubt the answer is 'yes'.

Now I wouldn't for one minute suggest that I've lived the life of a Hollywood movie A-lister, but I have seen a thing or two in my time – things which I would like to share with you now in a sort of 'greatest hits' run-down.

But before we begin, I'd just like to take a moment to make it clear that the list I am about to present to you isn't a 'top ten' in any official sense – I haven't polled anyone other than myself and, on occasion, my wonderful sister-in-law Gwen. It's also important to note that, despite the title indicating that everything on the list can (and should!) be 'done', there are one or two entries that are 'looking only' – you aren't required to 'do' anything. But, to my eye, the title 'Bryn's Top Ten Things To Do And/Or Have Someone Look At' is too wordy and, besides, I did spend quite a while getting the words of the current title exactly in the centre and looking right.

Safety briefing aside, we're ready for takeoff!
So hold on tight and off we go!

1) SEND AN EMAIL

I know what you're thinking – why is this top of the list? Well firstly, it's not – the list is in no particular order and so that number '1' is more for ease of reference than anything else – and secondly, you'd better get used to surprizes. There may be more coming.

Now, I am aware that some of you will be well ahead of me on this and may have sent a dozen or so emails already. But if you haven't, get yourself down to the local internet cafe and 'log on' (use a computer). You can send an email to anyone you please – send two if you like! – because (and here's the thing) they're absolutely free – no stamps required! And instant! And how many other things in this world have both of those qualities? So go on, email someone you love them. Email someone you hate them. Email anyone anything. It's free!

2) GO FOR DINNER – INSIDE YOUR OWN CAR!

No, I don't mean save your packed lunch for the evening rush hour, I mean visit a 'drive-thru' restaurant! It's a restaurant (usually one serving fast foods) where the waiters note down your order, take payment AND deliver your chosen dishes all through the (open) window of your car! That's 5-star service in my book. Convenience and entertainment are two of my favourite pastimes and 'drive-thru' dining has both in abundance. There's at least one such restaurant in Wales (at Culverhouse Cross, on the outskirts of Cardiff) and most likely several more. So what are you waiting for?

3) STONEHENGE

Magnificent! Breathtaking! Just some of the words I heard other people using when I went to see it. Who built it? No one knows. What was it for? No one knows. How did they lift those heavy stones? No one knows. Which begs the question, why do they need an information centre? I always did enjoy looking at pictures of this miracle of masonry, but it wasn't 'till I got the chance to visit in person a year or two ago that I realized just how much it looks like the photographs. A fantastic sight, I can assure you.

This is one of those entries in my top 10 where it's really more about 'looking' than 'doing'. Particularly as you can no longer get right up to the stones thanks to some nefarious activity in the recent past by a druid (the Information Centre is very instructive in this respect).

4) TRY ONE OF GWEN'S OMELETTES

This is only really of use if you are in, or planning to pass through, the Barry area (Wales, UK) – and in that case I'd ask you please to phone ahead instead of simply turning up unannounced. But you'll be heartily rewarded for your effort, I can assure you! Gwen's omelettes are second to none and their position at number '4' in my top ten is no reflection on their quality. As I've already stated, the numbering system is for ease of reference only.

5) TAKE A POWER SHOWER

Hygiene is very important to me and I shower at least once a day – sometimes twice. But no shower I have ever used has topped my 'power shower' experience. Snorkel optional! If, like me, you've grown accustomed to the traditional shower attachment to your bath taps, then you're in for a treat. Not only are they powerful (as the name suggests) but you can also change the pattern of the water. You can have 'normal', 'massage' or both together! Fascinating. They're expensive and awkward to fit at home, but I understand some of the more modern hotels now offer power showers – so if I were you, I'd find your nearest and book a slot. Half an hour should suffice – you'll come out feeling fresh as a daisy and ready for anything.

6) PARAGLIDING

I've been rather cajoled into including this one by my new nephew-in-law. It's a form of sport and, truth be told, I'm still not entirely sure how it works but I do know it involves a sort of parachute jump where, instead of falling to earth, you get towed into the sky by a boat (which is not in the air, but on a body of water some way below). What happens before and after that is anyone's guess.

I'd have to put this item firmly in the category of 'ones to watch' rather than actually do.

7) GET FIT

Regular exercize, lots of fresh air and a healthy diet – it may not sound like fun, but by golly you'll feel great! And 'working out' (as it's now called) can even become something to look forward to if you partner up with a 'buddy'. So grab a friend, start pumping away and teach your body who's boss!

I realize this may be incompatible with item 2 on the list.

8) RIDE IN A SPORTS CAR

Ah, now this one's quite interesting because it's not something I've ever actually done. But, assuming it was on a suitable racing circuit, in a car driven by a certified professional and with medical expertize on hand should anything go wrong and with the car going at no more the 70mph (the maximum speed limit in this country) then I think I might rather enjoy it. The car would ideally be a swanky-looking convertible, but with roll bars and side impact bars for safety.

9) A TRIP TO MADAME TUSSAUDS

Imagine shaking hands with David Beckham before turning the corner and coming face to face with Robin Williams! Well, there's a place where you can do exactly that! It's deep in the heart of London and is a sort of museum of people – famous people from the world of television, film and America who, were it not for the fact they are unflinching and stood perfectly still, you might easily mistake for the real thing! And here's the mindboggling thing – they're all made of wax. Wax! Every single one. It beggars belief, it really does. I even got to squeeze Brad Pitt's bottom – without fear of arrest!

10) LIVE IN WALES

I know I'm biased, but Wales really is a smashing place to live. It really is. I realize this item is more a long-term objective than a brief activity, but I'd still put it firmly in the category of 'things to do'. Sure, you can visit Wales with ease these days – the M4 is a wonderful stretch of road and even the train service is finally improving – but nothing can quite make up for settling down here for good. Home is where the heart is and mine's in Barry (Island).

So there you have it. I'd be interested to know if anyone reading has managed all ten. Or you may very well have your own top ten. If you do – and there's no reason why you shouldn't – then let's discuss them. Man to man. Go with your computer to MySpace and you'll find me there.

29th February 2007

Dearest Nessa,

Seeing as you are refusing my calls and wouldn't even answer the door to me when I drove all the way to see you, I have no option but to send you this letter.

Since you left, I just don't know what to do with myself. I've just been walking round in a daze, comfort eating. Last night I had two Viennettas and a packet of bourbons, but afterwards I just felt worse. To be honest with you, Nessa, I brought them straight back up again. If you don't get back with me I feel this might just be the start of a slippery slope.

I'll do whatever it takes to get you back. If you preferred using my jag, we can swap! I could sort your council tax out for you, no questions asked! I'll stop wearing my socks during physical relations! Whatever it takes, Nessa, just name it!

You're a very special lady, Nessa Jenkins. You do things to me that no other woman has ever done. Literally. And what's making the split worse is that I keep noticing little things that remind me of you; birdsong in the morning, sunset over Westminster, a toilet brush. Take me back, Ness! Take me back and I promise everything will be okay.

I'll be waiting next to the burger van in Barry at 7pm on Saturday. If you're there, then I'll be having twelve burgers, then two fingers for dessert.

Love you always,

John Prescott

Thursday 11th August

What a day! Glorious sunshine with barely a cloud in the sky until well after 7pm. Barely a nibble all morning until — score! I hooked a beautiful-looking rainbow trout shortly after 3:17pm (by my wrist watch which I set with the clock on Teletext) and, with Jason's help, reeled him in. He really is a cracking lad — and surprisingly nimble. So, thanks to some grade-A team work, we had ourselves a cracking roast trout for our tea! I for one am thoroughly enjoying myself up here and I'm thrilled to say Jason has taken to fishing like a natural!

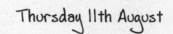

Friday 12th August

Re-reading Thursday's entry, I realize
I missed a trick. What a fool! What I
should have written was 'Jason has taken
to fishing like a FISH TO WATER'!
Must remember to email that one to my
e-pal Tony when I get back. Jason thinks
it's very funny and he's got such a lovely
laugh. Can't write for long because we're
in our tent now and I think my torchlight
is keeping Jason awake, as is my talking
out loud. It's been a long day and not
as successful as yesterday. Cloud.

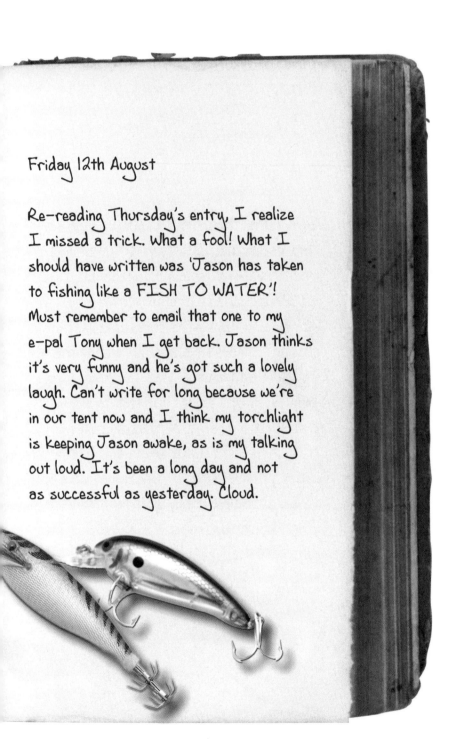

Saturday 13th August

Saturday the 13th!! Unlucky for some! And especially us intrepid fishermen it would seem. I somehow managed to cut my finger whilst preparing my hook this morning. Thanks to some quick thinking by Jason, cream was applied from the first-aid bum bag and I was bandaged up in no time. I'm not embarrassed to admit I did shed a tear, but Jason saw me right in no time with another of his Elton John impressions. They're uncanny. It's lovely to be spending some quality time with him. I've got to go, Jason's signalling that our soup has reached the boil. Mmm!

Monday 15th August

I can't sleep. I've got no
appetite. And I'm still finding
bits of that soup ... everywhere.
What a mess. What a mess.

On the plus side, Achmed came
round for tea this evening. He
told me that they're thinking
about making an iPod that's also
a phone! Feeling better after
hearing that news. Bet they'll call
it a podPhone or something very
similar! Wonder if you'll be able
to play music over the phone?

My Computer

Spreadsheets

Office

LIBRARY
🎵 Music
🎬 Movies
🖥 TV Shows
📻 Podcasts
📶 Radio
🔔 Ringtones

▼ PLAYLISTS
🎲 Party Shuffle
⚙ Top Ten Played
⚙ Recently Added
🎵 Nessa's Birthing Songs
🎵 Music For The Car
🎵 Gwen's song
🎵 Bryn's Workout
🎵 Back up of Gwen's song

Now Playing

Goo

	Name	Artist
1	Goodbye My Lover	James Blunt
2	You're Beautiful	James Blunt
3	Wise Men	James Blunt
4	Carry You Home	James Blunt
5	1973	James Blunt
6	Guide Me Now O'Grea...	Fron Male Voice Cl
7	A Million Love Songs	Take That
8	Life On Mars	David Bowie
9	Bohemian Rhapsody	G4
10	Gangster Trippin'	Fat Boy Slim

23 songs, 70 minutes

Start

View

Search

Jamie really does have a cracking voice. I'll be honest with you, I do like to sing along to this in the car. But I do keep the volume down so that I can hear any approaching emergency vehicles.

Who's this song about? Well it could be about Gwen, Stace or Nessa. But no. It's about the casting director of the Harry Potter films, Dixie Chassay! Her and Blunt used to be an item, you see.

A lovely song about wise men near the sea. Although it is rather spoilt by the use of the S-H-1-T word 36 seconds in. (0:36)

This song makes me think of Stace – when she was a kid I often had to carry her home. Particularly when she was tired. It's almost as if he knows what I'm thinking! He's such a nice bloke. I've never heard anyone say a bad word about him. As she got older, Nessa used to carry her home when she'd had a bit too much 'pop'.

This song is so new that I actually downloaded it directly to my computer! Apparently it is even possible to copy that downloaded mp3 to a cassette tape so that you can play it in the car! Not that the Picasso has a cassette player, but my last car did.

I bet the man who wrote this did not expect it to end up in mp3 format! But it has. Perhaps in the future all the hymns won't be in 'hymn books' but on 'hymn mp3 players'!

It was played at our Stacey's wedding. And when I think of that day it always brings a tear to my eye. Best day of my life. Give it ten years and most iPods will probably be able to hold a million love songs. Imagine that!

If I was on Stars in Their Eyes I would definitely be David Bowie. His music really does make you think. For example – is there life on Mars? It's unlikely.

The G4 boys bring a very modern twist to an old classic. You know what would be really amazing? It would be amazing if G4, wait for it … covered a James Blunt song! It might, perhaps, be the best cover version of all time.

Dick Powell put this track on here when he was showing me how to 'rip' or 'copy' a CD to my computer. It's not my favourite, but I have to say, it is growing on me.

🔊 Computer ⬦   Burn Disc   👁   ⏏

Bryn's

Lyrics & Meanings

I'm going to tell you something. There's nothing I like more than plugging my iPod into the Citroen Picasso's mp3 connector, sticking on my playlist of sing-along car songs and belting out a few hits to whomever I happen to be chauffeuring. Thing is, now and again I find myself singing lyrics to a popular song without really thinking about what they mean. Sometimes you can have a sudden realization that shocks you to the core – like when I stopped to think about what a 'Milkshake' was and exactly why it brought all the boys to the yard. So I've had a sit down and I've tried to think about what the words mean in some of my favourite songs.

JAMES BLUNT – WISE MEN

Well I've got myself into a right pickle with this one. 'Look who's alone now, it's not me, it's not me'; well clearly James feels that when all's been said and done, he's in a better position than the three wise men he's been talking about, because he's not alone. Perhaps he's found a girlfriend, or a wife, or a pet of some kind. However – and this really doesn't make any sense – then James sings, 'Those three wise men have got a semi by the sea'. So clearly they are not alone now either, are they? Each of them has two other wise men to keep them company. So James has got no reason to gloat about having company. Perhaps those three wise men are just three guys who happen to get on and for whatever reason, they aren't interested in getting married so they bought a house together. Maybe that's the only way they could get on the property ladder. He's got a cracking voice though, hasn't he?

JACK JOHNSON – BETTER WHEN WE'RE TOGETHER

What a lovely song. Not as bitter as James Blunt, this fellow. 'There's no combination of words I could put on the back of a postcard.' It seems Jack Johnson is a bit worried that he's simply not eloquent enough to articulate the love he has for his girlfriend. Well I beg to differ, Jack! You've got an dazzling way with words, you silly-billy! Forget postcards, this boy could probably write a really lovely novel full of lovely imagery of mango trees and sepia tone photographs. Perhaps one reason I like this song so much is that I have a couple of sepia tone photographs in my album (thanks to a setting on my digital camera that does them). Not sure it's working though as they just come out all brown. Regardless, Jack Johnson is a lovely lad and I'm sure he'll have no problem wooing the young lady he's singing about.

MICHAEL JACKSON – BAD

Well this one's pretty simple to work out, isn't it? We've all read a fair bit about Michael Jackson in the papers and this is just him putting his hands up and acknowledging he might have been a bit out of control on occasion. He's saying 'I'm bad' and also that we know it. Fair enough – none of us can condone what may or may not have happened, but at least the boy isn't trying to wriggle out of it. When he sings 'The word is out, you're doin' wrong, gonna lock you up, before too long', I think that's probably one of his brothers, maybe Tito, having a gentle word with him about it all. And it obviously worked because he's managed to stay out of jail and on the straight and narrow, hasn't he?

QUEEN – BOHEMIAN RHAPSODY

Well, I don't really know where to start with this. Those Queen boys must have been out of their faces when they wrote it! Obviously not when they wrote the music, though. You'll often hear me say this to people, but I would say that Bohemian Rhapsody, musically, is up there with any classical music you can think of. I can only assume that Freddie, Brian and the boys must have been so chuffed with the music part that they indulged in a celebratory drink or twenty – and only then did they get cracking on the lyrics. That's why there's all those fandangos, bismillahs, guns, heads, silhouettos and scaramouches. If only Jack Johnson had been around – he could have put some lovely sentiments to their tune.

EBENEEZER GOODE – THE SHAMEN

I'm afraid I'm not going to write much about this one as I don't want to give it the oxygen of publicity. Suffice it to say, after nearly a decade of me heartily singing along to this jolly tale of a Victorian eccentric, Nessa finally pointed out that it contains some very well concealed subliminal messages. I have not listened to it since, nor will I listen to it again any time soon. The Shamen have disappointed me.

WHEN YOU SAY NOTHING AT ALL – RONAN KEATING

Now there are two ways of interpreting 'You say it best when you say nothing at all'. The first possibility is that Ronan's saying that his girlfriend (or wife) doesn't need to say that she loves him, because the way that she looks at him and behaves around him means there are no need for words. Her love need not be spoken for it is obvious to the whole world just how much she adores Ronan. The other interpretation is that the girlfriend (or wife) might have a grating voice or perhaps a speech impediment of some description. She may even have a strong regional accent which makes it hard for him to take her seriously. Therefore Ronan finds her more attractive when she's silent and this song is his way of breaking that news to her, but with a positive spin. I hope it's the first, more romantic possibility myself. Though, given the way Ronan treated those lovely Boyzone lads when he went solo, I would not be at all surprized if it were the second option.

John,

First things first. I changed the locks, okay? So stop trying to use your old key. The neighbours keep saying they can hear crying outside in the night and it's only a matter of time before someone uses their camera phone to make a tidy bit of cash from the papers. I'm telling you this for your own good. I sleep through it myself.

I'm not gonna lie to you, we had some good times. Watching the smile on your face at those all you-can-eat buffets in Chinatown. Summer days playing croquet on your lawn. Winning game after game of doubles tennis against David Blunkett and his bitch.

But in our heart of hearts, I think we always both knew it couldn't last. We're just too different. You came from a working-class family in a Welsh coastal town and spent much of your youth working in the merchant navy and taking part in boxing contests. Whereas I ... well, actually, we pretty much grew up the same. If I'm bein' honest with you, that's a bad example. But my point is that the chemistry just isn't there. You're just not enough for me, John. That's nobody's fault, it's just the way it is.

I'm genuinely sorry to hear about your eating problems, but at the end of the day, you can't lay that on me. That's for you to deal with. All I can do is offer you the same advice I gave to Lady Di; eat less, vom less.

Tidy, Nessa

PS. I know you still have three of my thongs. Please send them back. Washed.

3 March, 2007

Dear Nessa,

Although you may not remember me, I'm writing to you with a really big favour to ask. I'm Dewi Davies, the manager of Goldie Lookin' Chain. As you may have noticed, things have gone a little bit quiet on the GLC front. Obviously the boys were going great guns back in 04/05 and then when Maggot got 3rd place in Celebrity Big Brother then we all thought we were going to be quids in.

However, the lads haven't troubled the charts in a while and I'm concerned that if something don't happen soon, they might have to go back to working at Caerphilly Morrisons (Eggsy's already doing evenings).

So anyways, last week, we had a summit meeting and I tried to find out why the lads stopped producing top thirty hits like in the good old days. After a bit of soul searching, they finally opened up and said that back then, their classic tracks such 'Your Mother's got a Penis' and 'Your Missus is a Nutter' were inspired by a muse. That muse is you, Nessa.

The boys said that when you drove the tour bus for them, they were at their most productive. They told me that without you, they're just not interested in making music any more. They miss you bad. Maggot's now saying that the only reason he did Big Brother was to try and get you out of his head. It didn't work. Ness, they all say that you're the only person they could ever love.

So please Nessa, please think about driving the bus on our upcoming tour. With your help, I really think we can get the boys back where they belong – the top 30.

Yours hopefully,

Dewi Davies

NESSA'S

Penny Arcade 'Systems'

A few years on and behind the slot machines has given me quite a strong understanding of how these flashing electronic beasts work. So I've developed a few systems that help you win all the time, every time. Don't get me wrong, I wouldn't encourage you to use these. Gambling's wrong and, I'll be honest, it can be a homewrecker. If only Paul Merson had spent more time on his football training and less on the Barry Pleasure Park's fruities. But here's the methods to make the most out of these arcade systems. Don't go round blabbing that I told you how to do this. Alrigh'?

CLASSIC METHOD –
FOR USE ON ALL FRUITIES

Plain and simple. Alls you have to do is sit and watch as people plough money in to the machine. I'm not joking – after a few times round you will see how often it pays out. Then it's a simple waiting game. Watch as the muppets pour away their hard earned cash then, when enough has been put in, try your luck. I bet you'll only need to spend £3 to see a massive pay-out come your way. But I'll be honest, if I catches you doing it on my watch, you'll be out on your arse before you can blink.

JAPANESE SLOT MACHINES METHOD

The great things about the Japanese manufactured slot machines is that they all have an in-built cheat so I'm told. Dead simple. Wait five seconds. Hit hold. Wait five seconds. Hit hold. Wait five seconds. Hit hold. Bingo. Quids in. I haven't tried waiting ten seconds. Or twenty seconds. I'll be honest, I don't have the money to be wasting on things like that. I wouldn't take a gamble like that. I only gambles on sure fire wins.

'EASTENDERS MEGA MONEY BONANZA' METHOD

If you can find an 'Eastenders Mega Money Bonanza' fruity, and there aren't so many about nowadays, then this is a sure fire winner. Just count the seconds between Babs' laughs. If they're nine seconds apart, it's not worth touching. But if she's cackling every 12 seconds – you might as well go for it – 'cos she will be paying out a hefty wad. Why do the manufacturers build in these little quirks, you ask? 'Cos they top up their pay by going round winning money off their own fruit machines. Obvious now, isn't it?

CHANGE MACHINE METHOD

I've not tried this one, so don't take my word for it. But apparently, if you get a tenner, remove the creases, place it on a table with the Queen facing you, fold the bottom right corner, cut a 5mm slit about 14mm up from the bottom, warm it on the radiator for 8 minutes, wet the Queen's face and then stick it in to the change machine – it'll confuse the sensor and the machine will give your change as well as giving you the tenner back. You can only do this on the machine that gives out 2ps in change. So if you get any of the steps even slightly wrong it won't work and you'll be left with a pocket full of coppers. Try it if you want, but at the end of the day, it's you who'll have to bag them up and take them to the bank if it goes wrong.

10 PENCE PUSHER METHOD

If you rock 'em? It sets the alarm off. If you kick 'em? It sets the alarm off. If you try and reach through the slot? It sets the alarm off. If you put any coin other than a 10p in? It sets the alarm off. So how do you get in to these impenetrable fortresses? Think about it. Simplest trick. Wait till the machine attendant has gone on her/his break. Then reach into/kick/rock the machine to your heart's content. Yes the alarm will go off, but who's going to stop you? An attendant's tea break is her/his personal time and they will not get up for anyone. Not even thieves. It's not exactly a Derren Brown system, but it works.

THE KEY LOCK METHOD

If, like me, you have the keys to all of the machines then it's dead simple. Don't get me wrong, I don't steal the money. I does, however, open up the machine and press the button that increases the frequency that it pays out. Then when I plays it's much easier to win. But it's legit. And don't let no-one else tell you otherwise.

QUIZ MACHINE METHOD

When it comes to quiz machines, there's one simple system. Just be dead clever. If you know the answers to all the questions, you can't lose. However, if you ain't too smart, then there's only one bit of advice I can give you. Don't play quiz machines in clever places – the boffins will have won all the money you won't stand a chance. So that rules out Cambridge, Oxford, Mensa Social Functions or Stephen Fry's local boozer. Whereas, and I don't mean to regionally offend anybody by saying this, but it's always worth trying your luck if you're passing through Swindon.

'I remember my first wedding day. I woke up, in Vegas – didn't know where I was. Looked 'round – I was in bed with two of Gladys Knight's Pips.' Nessa,

Dear Goldie Lookin' Chain,

Alrigh' lads, what's occurring? As it's been a while, I s'pose I ought to start by congratulating Maggot on 3rd place in Celebrity Big Brother. Well done, I'm happy for you. I can't tell a lie though, Mags - you'd have been the first one out the house if I hadn't been working in that phone-vote counting centre, so you owes me one. As do Ant and Dec, for that matter.

Anyways, while I've missed your comedy hip-hop music from the airwaves in the last couple of years, I must say I haven't missed driving you bunch of twats around. Sure, we had some good times, like that England match when I suggested you dedicate 'You're Missus Is A Nutter' to Posh Spice. But that ain't enough, is it?

At the end of the day, I can't be having a relationship with eight of you at once. I know that you guys don't mind sharing me amongst yourselves for the rest of your days, but that just ain't my thing. I'm a one man girl. I've got too much loving in me to split eight ways.

It might be the case that you need me to make good music. But I can't just go around getting back with everyone who I inspired musically, just to help their careers. Though if I did then Chesney Hawkes would have been around a lot longer. You'll have to find your own direction. My advice is to look within yourselves, and just maybe you'll find some spoof raps lurking down there in your souls somewhere.

So it's a no from me. Good luck with the comeback tour though, fellas. And if it just ain't happening, then can I suggest Waitrose in Barry. They pay better than Morrisons and their pension scheme is highly regarded in the retail industry.

Laterz, Nessa

COACH HIRE

> *More smiles per gallon than any other bus in Barry.*

We'll get you there ... if we possibly can

DAVE'S COACHES

Pride Of Barry!

Get away from it all with Dave's Coach Tours. Affordable day trips for young and old. New destinations for 2009 include:

➤ **Bangor Gnome Sanctuary** – lots and lots of gnomes. Absolutely cracking if you like gnomes.

➤ **Weston Super-Mare Woollen Zoo** – a zoo of wool. Woollen giraffes, woollen elephant, woollen pig, woollen panda, woollen monkeys, woollen snake, woollen hippo, woollen bats, woollen deer, woollen bear, woollen ostrich, woollen zebra, etc.

➤ **Begg Pit** – Somerset's last remaining nutmeg mine. See how it used to be done!

➤ **Swindon**

Or why not create your own itinerary? Tailored day-trips available (state whether you prefer gnomes, wool, nutmeg or Swindon). Travel in style in a state-of-the art 42-seater coach offering the very best in luxury travel:

· **Wheels** · Comfy seat · **Air-conditioned windows** · Seatbelts (except seat 8) · **PA/Karaoke system** · Spare tyre, jack & warning triangle · **Cup holders (except seat 8)** · 2007/08 UK-wide super-scale road map (1in = 1km) · **TV with DVD player** · Small selection of adult DVDs · **Curtain (except seat 8)** · HGV-licenced and STD-free driver · **3rd party insurance, road tax & full MOT** · Smoking area (seat 8). No crack.

All parties welcome (no DSS, no school kids). Girls go for £1. You can't find us on the internet. To book – please speak to Dave in person (I don't have a phone). Tours available all year round (excluding Christmas Day, Boxing Day, Christmas Eve, New Year's Eve, New Year's Day, Easter Day, Palm Sunday, Bank Holiday weekends, weekends and May 10th).

SOUTH GLAMORGAN POLIC

WANTED. CA

VANESSA SHANESSA JENKINS

Do not approach or attempt to detain this
woman. She is extremely dangerous.

APPEAL FOR ASSISTANCE

N YOU HELP?

Subject is wanted in relation to crimes throughout the South Glamorgan region, including:

• Street performance without a valid license
• Possession of Class A Narcotics
• Possession of Class B Narcotics
• Possession of Class C Narcotics
• Running a Tattoo Parlour without a valid license
• Forging a Tattoo Parlour license
• Offering cash for questions to a prominent MP
• Running a Tattoo Parlour with a forged license
• 3 counts of indecent assault with a toilet brush
• Theft from Barry Island Pleasure Park (£25,000 in 1p and 2p pieces)

It is possible that Vanessa Jenkins may have altered her appearance to avoid detection. If this is the case, she may now look like one of these images:

Barry Island pleasure park are offering a cash reward for information on this suspect: £5000 (in 1p and 2p pieces)

If you have any information please call the
Barry Town Crime Busters Hotline

0801 789 321

Nessa's

Book Reviews

Satanic Verses
By Salman Rushdie

I won't lie, this one's a tough read. It put me through the wringer. At the end of the day though, when all's said and done, old Salman has got quite an imagination. He writes himself into some wonderful situations and then writes himself straight back out of them again. That said, if he was that good at writing, he'd have written himself out of his fatwa as well. This book's a heavy read and I suspect you won't fancy reading it a second time. In fact, the idea of reading it twice is about as sensible as Salman doing a book signing in Tehran.

Was this review helpful to you?   YES   NO

Prezza: My Story: Pulling No Punches
By John Prescott

Well John-John's put a lot of meaty stuff into this, but thank God there's a lot of meat he's left out too. I was glad to see that, as I requested, he made no mention of me in there. No need to upset Pauline any more than she needs to be. And while I'm not embarrassed by anything we got up to, I think that John's reputation would never recover if he had told the whole truth. It's a good read, but not as revealing as it was hanging out with him, Blunkett and Blunkett's bitch.

Was this review helpful to you?   YES   NO

Spycatcher
By Peter Wright

Back in the day, I was a spook for a good couple of years and this book is, quite frankly, a load of bollocks. There are much, much worse things going on in MI5 but I, along with my colleagues (both alive and dead), have signed the official secrets act so my mouth remains tightly shut.

Was this review helpful to you?

Enduring Love
By Ian McEwan

Some people say he's Britain's best living novelist, but no word of a lie I think that's over-egging it a bit. Sure, he can write a solid story, but at the end of the day, he don't even give Martin Amis a run for his money. Anyways, this one's about a fella who's a bit of a stalker, so I could relate to it. Problem I had though was that my exes were much worse stalkers than the bloke in this story. This guy's a lightweight compared to them so the book never really done it for me. I lent it to Richard Madeley and he liked it and was going to tell all his pals about it. 'So,' I says, 'if you likes it so much, why not tell your audience? Start a national book club.' Not a bad idea as it turns out.

Was this review helpful to you?

Trainspotting
By Irvine Welsh

What a bloody lame story. If them jocks think they're wild, they should come down Barry and hang out here for a bit. Our scagheads put them to shame. I know that ain't nothing to be proud of, but if they want a junkie competition then they can have one. And they'll lose, bad.

Was this review helpful to you?

Mick's

Golfing Tips

Some men will tell you golf has two big hazards: sand and water. But if, like me, you've been married for thirty years then you'll know there's a third hazard that'll knacker more rounds than the other two put together: the wife.

Golf is a game of skill, judgement and approach – and never more so when you're handling the missus. Knowing how to squeeze in a round or two a week without her noticing will save you a lot of grief – and missed tee-off times.

So here are my top ten golfing tips for a simpler life – I've made the mistakes so you don't have to. Isn't it about time you started spending more of your time in the clubhouse than you do in the doghouse?

• **WEAR SUNSCREEN.** Not to avoid skin cancer, though that is a nice little side effect. Nothing says 'I've been out on the greens all afternoon' like a sunburnt bonce and a tanned right hand. I learnt that one the hard way.

• **BUY YOUR CLUBS SECOND HAND.** Women are like magpies and can spot shiny new kit at fifty paces. But if she does catch a glimpse of your golf bag, she's less likely to twig that £120 charge on the credit card was for an oversized 3-wood if your new club's already covered in mud.

• **IF YOUR DRIVES START PULLING RIGHT,** try standing the tee further back in your stance, open the club face slightly and try to shake off that nagging feeling that your wife's hiding in the bushes somewhere, watching your every move.

• **MENTHOL LOCKETS** are the best thing for getting rid of beer-breath after a shandy or two at the 19th hole. They're better than mints and have the added advantage of making it appear you have a cold – which would explain why you're home from work an hour earlier than normal.

• **DON'T WATCH GOLF ON THE BOX** when the wife's around. The moment she realizes 'birdie', 'eagle' and 'woods' are all golfing terms, it becomes much harder to pretend you were discussing ornithology with your mates when she walks in on you unexpectedly.

• **WHEN FACED WITH A SHORT CHIP ONTO THE GREEN,** leave the pitching wedge in the bag for a change and try a little tap with a four-iron – it'll make light work of even the wettest green. Just don't over-hit or you'll be there all night and you don't need me to tell you what sort of trouble you'll be in if you're not home in time for supper.

• **USE WOOLLY HEAD-COVERS** on all your clubs. It won't make a blind bit of difference to your game but, since they muffle the clanging sound, you'll find it much easier to sneak your bag out of the car boot and back into the house without the wife noticing.

• **GET INTO THE HABIT** of letting your phone run out of charge on a regular basis. That way, when you switch the thing off and leave it in the glove box while you play a round, the missus won't get suspicious. She'll just think you're an idiot. Keep it that way.

• **WATCHING THE PROS IS DAUNTING,** but spend time mastering three or four different shots and your game will improve no end. Likewise, spend time mastering three or four different excuses for why you're not home on time (again) and there'll start to sound more and more convincing.
Never, ever arrange to play a round on your wife's birthday. Unless it's a weekday, in which case you might be able to fit in nine holes mid-morning.

From: PAM
Date: 11-Jun-08 12:50 pm

Hurry home Charles, Camilla is ready and waiting for you!

Reply   More

11-Jun-08 12:50 pm

From: MICK
I'm in an afternoon session with Woodruffe. Not at my desk so call the mobile if you need to. Be back at 6.30. Mick

Reply   More

From: PAM
Date: 11-Jun-08 12:50 pm

Michael Shipman. You'd better enter into the spirit of things, else they'll be no tea for you let alone anything else.

Reply   More

11-Jun-08 12:57 pm

From: MICK
Pam! Give me a break! I'm in a meeting for God's sake. Woodruffe's right next to me.

Reply   More

11-Jun-08 12:58 pm

From: MICK
Pam! Come on!

Reply   More

11-Jun-08 12:59 pm

From: MICK
It's always been you, Camilla. As soon as I get back, I'll wear the ears. And nothing else.

Reply   More

From: PAM
Date: 11-Jun-08 12:50 pm

Oh Charles! I want you now! I want you to take me like you did on our honeymoon in Balmoral!

Reply   More

From: MICK
Sorry Camilla. I meant, I have a visit to a youth project that's been funded by my Prince's Trust. They're helping inner city kids to learn computer skills. Back at 6.30. Love Charles.

11-Jun-08 12:53 pm
12:54 pm

Reply   More

From: PAM
Date: 11-Jun-08 12:50 pm

Charles, I can't wait. Please! Tell me! What are you going to do to me when you get back here to Buckingham Palace? Camilla

12:52 pm

Reply   More

From: MICK
I'm going to tell you about my day, then we can have tea, then there's Champion's League and after that we can go 'upstairs'. Love Charles.

11-Jun-08 12:55 pm
12:56 pm

Reply   More

From: PAM
Date: 11-Jun-08 12:50 pm

Forget it, Michael. You're not even trying.

12:52 pm

Reply   More

From: MICK
Traffic's bad at Brentwood so won't be back till more like 8. Keep my tea warm. Charles

11-Jun-08 7:21 pm
7:23 pm

Reply   More

From: PAM
Date: 11-Jun-08 12:50 pm

That's it, Charles. You're sleeping on the Buckingham Palace living room sofa tonight.

12:52 pm

Reply   More

12:52 pm

Names   Go to

7:23 pm

Reply   More

SAY NO TO THE MAST!

Your help is urgently required to save the brains of our children!

We have received alarming information that Augur Communications will soon be erecting a mobile phone mast within 68 feet of our homes (or even closer if you have a conservatory). As you are probably aware, microwaves from mobile phone masts have been scientifically linked to many serious problems including; children getting brain tumours, pigeons that land on them being instantly killed, people's heads feeling hotter and uncooked chicken becoming cooked.

Someone's got to do something about it! If we work together we can abate the tide of phone masts being put up in this area! So join us ~~mast abaters~~ in the field behind Lime Tree Avenue for a silent protest. There will be live acoustic music and a barbecue serving burgers and quality local sausages.

If you would like to join the Billericay Against Phonemasts Society then please contact Pamela Shipman by either emailing (pamela@baps.com) or on her mobile (07700 900 436), though the reception is ridiculous so it's probably best using the email address.

NOT IN MY NAME

Display in window to show your support

G&S
ENGINEERING

Home

Profile

Mission Statement

Services

History

Legal

Location

Recruitment

Contacts

MICHAEL SHIPMAN BSc MechE
Company Director

Having started the company ten years ago we have collected a large loyal client base. Even though we are a big company it is important for us to give you the personal touch. That's why we think it would be good for you to get to know us. So let's learn a bit more about one of our directors – Michael Shipman.

If you recognize Michael, that's because he's a TV star – yet you wouldn't know it. Even though he's a celebrity, he is still a very down-to-earth, approachable guy.

Michael is a family man who likes to spend his recreational time on the golf course. In fact, he even spends some of his work time on the golf course too – striking deals and making big decisions with similar-minded clients, apparently.

Michael's great at leading the company and he's initiated several fantastic team-building schemes, including the ever-popular 'Staff Chef' day (last Friday of every month) in which a member of staff cooks a meal. He probably only set this up so he could show off his amazing marinaded lamb!

Here's what some of our clients say about him:

'Michael Shipman is very punctual.' Carla Rickman (Rudick Ltd.)

'You can always rely on Michael to pick up the phone within three rings. That's quality.' Tony Harris (B.E. Engineering LTD)

'Michael will do anything to help, be it problem solving, helping to increase margins or lending them a 5 iron.' Mark Stanton (Hudson & Stanton Repairs LTD)

'We feel privileged to be dealing with a bona fide television personality'. Jamie Edwards, J.U.R. Logistics

THE LIME TREE VOICE

Written for Lime Tree Avenue residents BY Lime Tree Avenue residents

STREET PARTY TIME!

By Pamela Shipman

The 9th of April is fast approaching and it's time once again to commemorate the marriage of Prince Charles to his true love, Camilla Parker-Bowles. It's a chance for all of us to celebrate the greatest love story of the century by having our annual street party.

As in previous years, I will be coordinating events and providing bunting and fold-up chairs and tables. Thanks to Pete for once again volunteering to man the barbecue. I'm sure many of you will have had a bit of Pete's sausage (hee hee) last time and enjoyed a taste of quality. Thanks also to Susan for offering to make the desserts – it's evident that she's been practising hard all year. Due to marital stress, Dawn does not feel capable of taking on the responsibility of collecting glassware from Sainsbury's. Therefore if any of you would like a chance to get involved with the street party committee then this is your opportunity! Simply send me an application letter with your name and address on it. Then complete the tie-breaker question in no more than 10 words; **'I think Camilla Parker-Bowles is our greatest royal asset because …'** **Judges' decision (my decision) will be final.**

Events will begin at 12.30 (the exact time the two love birds tied the knot back in '05) with a tribute speech to Charles and Camilla from myself. Food will follow immediately after at 1.30.

RECIPE AVENUE

This month, Michael Shipman from Number 17 shares his recipe for Marinaded Lamb.

Marinaded Lamb is really simple. Firstly, get some garlic, olive oil and rosemary and bash them all together in the pestle. Or the mortar. Whichever one the bowl is. Then massage the marinade into the joint and leave for an hour. Sounds like a dangerously long time, doesn't it? But hold your nerve. Let that marinade permeate through. Then bung it in the oven for 45 minutes. Once it's done, remove it from the oven with a pair of quality oven gloves (not a tea towel) and serve. Just wait till you taste the gravy!

Gavin Shipman of No. 17 and Stacey West from Barry Island in Wales have announced their engagement.

CLASSIFIEDS

 *Pam's*

Vegetarian Do's and Don'ts

Having seen the world through a vegetarian's eyes I now have a better idea of how those poor little animals must feel. In many ways I have always been a little bit vegetarian as I don't like to see animals suffer, apart from wasps, which is why I only eat animals that Hugh Fearnley-Whittingstall and Jamie Oliver have set free in their television programmes.

To make sure you don't miss out on normal food, vegetarian scientists have come up with three alternatives that can be made to look exactly like their meat equivalents. First of all there's Quorn, which is like nature's chameleon. It can look like any meat, but always smells like your fridge has gone off. Vegetarian sausages are very similar to meat sausages. So similar, in fact, that you've got to be very careful not to mix them up on the barbeque (else Mick will get in one of his strops). And finally there's tofu. This is a special type of vegetarian food as it can be eaten by non-vegetarians. It is best to hide tofu in a curry sauce or in a salad – that way there's no risk of you actually tasting it.

'Do you even care about the fact that we're all gonna die... of brain cancer and tumour-brains?' Pam

Many people say that being a veggie is unhealthy, but as a vegetarian you are in good company. Many celebrities don't eat meat, such as Linda McCartney and Bob Marley, and they turned out okay.

There is an extreme form of vegetarianism, and that's the 'vegan'. My friend Picky Vicky is one of these. She can't eat or drink anything that's come from an animal. For that matter, she can't eat gluten or nuts … and then she wonders why no one invites her to dinner parties. She should take a leaf out of Big Fat Sue's book and not be so fussy. However, some people call themselves vegetarians because they're trying to hide the fact they're fussy eaters. You can spot these people because they're the ones who eat fish.

There are two major downers to not eating meat. One is that you're supposed to eat lots of seeds and eggs to get your protein levels up. The second is that you live longer. Now, that may sound like a good thing, but getting so old that you have to stay permanently connected up to all those bleepy machines like they have on Casualty isn't my idea of fun at all. You certainly couldn't go fencing every Tuesday.

People think you shouldn't wear fur or leather if you're a vegetarian. But as far as I'm concerned it's a case of 'waste not, want not'. If a cow's already been killed, you might as well use every part of it and make some shoes and a jacket. Can you eat mink? If you can, then I think it's okay to make fur coats for rich people, 'cos then you can give the mink meat to starving people starving in the third world.

Christmas Omelette
-Eggs, Turkey, Roast Potatoes, Brussels Sprouts,
Parsnips, Carrots, Bread Sauce, Butter, Pepper.

Spicy Omelette
-Eggs, Jalapeno Peppers, Cayenne Peppers, Sweet Peppers,
Scotch Bonnet Peppers, Bell Peppers, Birdseye Chilli Peppers,
Butter, Pepper.

Tongue Twister
-Eggs, Pack Of Pickled Peppers, Butter, Pepper.

Double Omelette
-Eggs, Eggs, Butter, Butter, Pepper, Pepper.

Omelette De La Mere
-Eggs, Fish Fingers, Butter, Pepper.

Welsh Omelette
-Eggs, Leek, Butter, Pepper.

Chicken Tikka Omelette
-Eggs, Diced Chicken,
Lloyd Grossman's Curry Sauce,
Butter, Pepper.

Diet Omelette
-Eggs, Margarine, Pepper.

Perfect Size   Custard Omelette

Chocolate Omelette   Jelly Omelette
                          Chicken Korma Omelette

Ice Cream Omelette

SAVE
10%

When you spend £20 or more on eggs. Offer valid for 2 weeks only at participating stores in the Barry Island area.
One voucher per customer, while stocks last.

VALU-STORE

Plain Omelette
-Eggs, Butter.

Peppery Plain Omelette
-Eggs, Butter, Pepper.

Cheese Omelette
-Eggs, Cheese,
Butter, Pepper.

Cheese & Ham Omelette
-Eggs, Cheese, Ham Slice, Butter, Pepper.

L'omelette
-Eggs, Cheese (French), Ham Slice (French), Butter, Pepper.

Hawaiian Omelette
-Eggs, Cheese, Tinned Pineapple, Ham Slice, Butter, Pepper.

Spanish Omelette
-Eggs, Diced Onion, Sherry, Butter, Pepper.

Surf 'N' Turf Omelette
-Eggs, Seafood Sticks, Peperrami, Butter, Pepper.

Spomlette
-Eggs, Spam, Butter, Pepper.

Ome-lette me at it!

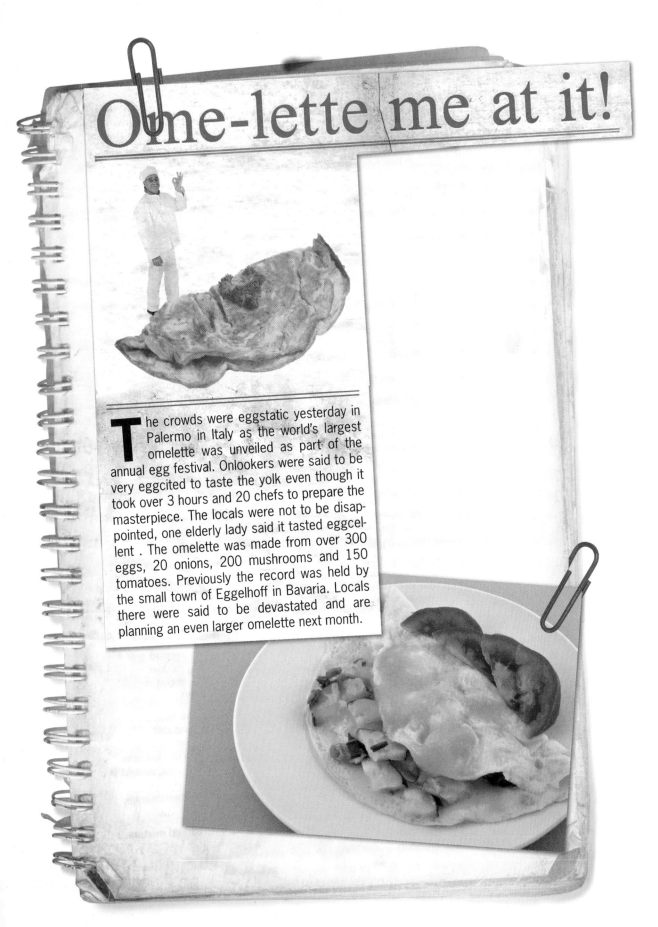

The crowds were eggstatic yesterday in Palermo in Italy as the world's largest omelette was unveiled as part of the annual egg festival. Onlookers were said to be very eggcited to taste the yolk even though it took over 3 hours and 20 chefs to prepare the masterpiece. The locals were not to be disappointed, one elderly lady said it tasted eggcellent . The omelette was made from over 300 eggs, 20 onions, 200 mushrooms and 150 tomatoes. Previously the record was held by the small town of Eggelhoff in Bavaria. Locals there were said to be devastated and are planning an even larger omelette next month.

TWIX TART

I think this is one of Delia's

INGREDIENTS
2lb Sweet Pastry
1 x 12inch Tart Ring
8oz Unsalted Butter
23 Twixes (Double Finger)

Pam,
It was lovely to have you and Mick over at the weekend. Glad you enjoyed yourselves and here's that recipe for the dessert we had, plus a couple more of my specialities thrown in for luck!
See you at Jujitsu,
Love,
Susan (Big Fat Sue)

1. Line the Tart Ring with your sweet pastry.
2. Put 17 of the Twixes (ie. 34 Twix fingers) and all of the butter the into a food processor and whiz it up until it becomes nice and squishy.
3. Take 6 heaped tables spoons of the mixture and put it into a separate bowl.
4. Put the remainder of the Twix mixture on top of the pastry. Spread it nice and neatly using a pallet knife.
5. Lick the excess mixture off the pallet knife using your tongue.
6. Cook the tart at 150C for 10 minutes.
7. While you are waiting for tart to cook, get a table spoon and start spooning the mixture you put aside into your mouth.
8. Allow the tart to cool completely
9. Garnish the tart with 7 Twixes (ie. 14 fingers) in a pattern of your choice. My preference is a lattice effect.
10. Eat the remaining Twix (ie. 2 fingers)
11. Serve with double cream, custard and chocolate sauce.

(NB. For my 'Kit-Kat Tart' use the same recipe as above but replace Twixes with double the amount of Kit-Kats. Or divide by two for Chunky Kit-Kat)

QUALITY STREET CHEESECAKE

I can't claim this one! It's copied straight out of 'Delia's Desserts'

INGREDIENTS

1 x 12inch Tart Ring
3 Packs Tesco Value Bourbons
1 x Christmas Size Tin of Quality Street
8oz Unsalted butter
16oz Cream Cheese
1 x Twix (2 fingers)

1. Crush up the bourbons, put them in a food processor and add the butter. Whiz it up until nice and squishy.
2. Line the base of the Tart Ring with butter then add this mix to form a cheesecake base.
3. Remove the Coconut Eclairs from the tin of Quality Street (blue wrappers) and dispose of them in your kitchen bin.
4. Wash up the food processor.
5. Mind your fingers on the sharp bits.
6. Dry the food processor with a tea towel.
7. Mind your fingers of the sharp bits.
8. Unwrap the rest of the Quality Streets and put them into the food processor with the cream cheese. Whiz it up until nice and squishy.
9. Pour the Quality Street mix onto the biscuit base.
10. Allow to cool in the fridge for at least an hour.
11. Eat the twix.

NESSA'S

Flag Collection

Something not a lot of people know about me is that I'm
a part-time vexillologist. And those that do know rarely
understand what it means. All it does mean is that I collects
flags – and I got hundreds. Some I loves, some I doesn't.
And there's even one or two I can't bring myself to look at
to this day. The Jolly Roger still gives me flashbacks to my
time in the Navy even now – suffice to say that while the
Caribbean is a lovely holiday destination to many, its seas
are still riddled with danger. Here's just a small selection.

GREECE

Stace bought this back from her honeymoon with Gav and from what she said it was a crackin'
country. I'd already got it (it's a basic for vexillologists), but didn't have the heart to tell her. I'd
love to visit Greece myself, but following a run-in with the Turkish half of Cyprus a year or two
back, I don't think I'd be very welcome. For now at least, the only Greece I'll be seeing is under
the hood of my wagon on a hard shoulder somewhere.

LIBYA

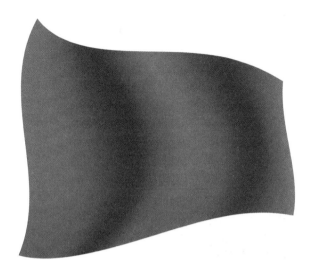

Granted, green is the colour of Islam and the Libyans are into all that big-time, but when you've made as much money from selling oil as they have, you'd expect something a bit more flashy than this. I'm not bein' funny, but if truth be told, this is terrible. The least favourite of my collection and I would have probably chucked it long ago if it weren't for the fact that it's the original.

IRAN

HUNGARY

The Iranians have been very good to me in the past, but this I can't abide. Taking a fuzzy Hungarian flag, turning it upside down and putting that thing in the middle isn't fooling anyone. Shocking.

CYMRU

What can I say? The king of the flags. Bold colours and a powerful emblem – makes me proud to be Welsh. Brings a smile to my face whenever I see it. I've got several of these in all shapes and sizes – including one drawn on a grain of rice by a toothless Chinaman I met on the Yellow River – but this one hangs in the back of the cab in my truck. It gets a mixed reception out on the roads, but my advice to you would be don't give me any grief. A lad in a Fiat Punto learnt that the hard way just last week.

SEYCHELLES

The wonderful people of the Seychelles gave me this flag when I introduced a new method of tuna fishing to the islands back in '86. It's a lovely piece but I won't pretend it's easy to hang – it clashes with nearly everything else in my collection.

UNITED KINGDOM

I've got nothing against the British, but when creating a flag to unite the nations of England, Scotland, Northern Ireland and Wales it'd be nice if you'd given just a nod to the Welsh. The crosses of St George, St Patrick and St Andrew are all in there – but what about St David? Didn't think anyone would notice, eh? Well, I have.

NEPAL

Brave people, the Nepalese. And you can see that in their flag – they're not interested in rectangles and coloured bands. But let me say this: when you're on the summit of Everest and the weather closes in, the strange shape of this flag makes it next to useless for conserving body heat. And I should know.

RICHARD,

I'M NOT BEING FUNNY BUT YOU WROTE THE LETTER ON HEADED 'JUDY & RICHARD SHOW' NOTE PAPER, SO THERE'S REALLY NO NEED TO SIGN OFF AS 'ANONYMOUS'.

NOW I'LL GET STRAIGHT TO THE POINT. I WAS CONVINCED THAT JUDY WAS ONLY YOUR TV WIFE, AND NOT YOUR ACTUAL WIFE. IF I'D HAVE KNOWN THIS YESTERDAY THEN I WOULDN'T HAVE LET THINGS GO THAT FAR. TO BE FAIR, YOU AND JUDY DON'T EVEN SHARE THE SAME SURNAME AND YOU MUST ADMIT THAT IS A BIT MISLEADING. THIS WAS SOMETHING YOU HAD THE OPPORTUNITY TO TELL ME IN NANDOS. OR, AT THE VERY LEAST, BEFORE WE LEFT YATES'S. BUT YOU FAILED TO DO SO.

IF YOU DON'T MIND, I HAVE A FEW COMMENTS ON LAST NIGHT'S SITUATION:

1) I'LL BE HONEST, YOUR ALI G IMPRESSION SHOULD BE EXCLUDED FROM THE BEDROOM. DON'T GET ME WRONG, YOU'VE GOT HIM DOWN TO A T (AND THAT'S SOMETHING TO BE PROUD OF) BUT I JUST DON'T BELIEVE THAT THE PHRASE 'BOOYA-KA-SHA' SHOULD BE USED AT THE POINT OF SEXUAL UNION.

2) I LOVE A BIT OF RAUNCHY CHAT DURING INTERCOURSE. BUT WHAT YOU DID THERE WAS PRACTICALLY AN INTERVIEW. THERE WAS ENOUGH PROBING GOING ON WITHOUT YOUR BARRAGE OF IN-DEPTH QUESTIONS. IF I'D WANTED PAXMAN BETWEEN THE SHEETS, I WOULDN'T HAVE STAYED AS QUIET AS I DID ON UNIVERSITY CHALLENGE. AND YOU CERTAINLY SHOULDN'T HAVE POINTED OUT WHO WAS 'COMING NEXT'. I DIDN'T FIND THAT HALF AS FUNNY AS YOU DID.

3) I TOOK YOUR RECOMMENDATION AND READ A THOUSAND SPLENDID SUNS. AND I DIDN'T LIKE IT. NOT MY CUP OF TEA. YES, KHALED HOSSEINI WRITES COMPELLINGLY FROM THE PERSPECTIVE OF A WOMAN, BUT TO BE FAIR IT DIDN'T FEEL MUCH DIFFERENT TO THE KITE RUNNER IN TONE. AS A RESULT, I HAVE DECIDED NOT TO ATTEND ANY MORE OF YOUR BOOK CLUBS. THANKS, BUT NO THANKS.

IN CONCLUSION: SINCE FINDING OUT THAT YOU ARE MARRIED, I HAVE NO INTEREST IN CONTINUING THIS RELATIONSHIP. AND I'LL ADD - DON'T WORRY ABOUT WHAT HAPPENED. IT HAPPENS TO MOST MEN. ALTHOUGH MOST MEN DON'T END UP CRYING ABOUT IT.   TIDY, NESSA

P.S. YOU'LL FIND YOUR VHS ENCLOSED. IT WAS A 120 MINUTE ONE, NOT 240 - DON'T FLATTER YOURSELF.

Billericay Herald

Wednesday, November 8, 2006   www.trickeybillericay.co.uk

Lucky Ducky

BY MARK JENKINS

Chris the duckling (pictured) had a lucky 'break' when he was discovered by a member of a local animal charity. 'I saw him by the side of a pond,' said Richard Cuthbertson, an RSPCA worker. 'It was apparent that the little fellow had broken his leg. We named him "Chris" because of his waddle!' Chris's leg was set in a splint made of lolly sticks and gauze. After three weeks of care, he was released back into his pond to rejoin his paddling pals. And you'll be happy to hear that this 'quackers' story has a happy ending. Not only is Chris's leg completely healed but also, as the RSPCA is a charity, Chris the duckling didn't have to pay the 'bill'! What a lucky ducky.

CONTROVERSY OVER CHURCH FÊTE CAKE BAKING CONTEST

More Inside...pg4

Body Found

BY ROB JENKINS

A Billericay company director stumbled across the last thing he expected to find when he came into work yesterday morning: a dismembered body. Michael Shipman, 53, arrived for a normal day at the office but instead he made a gory discovery. The charred and chopped corpse had been mutilated to such a degree that it still remains unidentified. 'It's the last thing you expect to find when you come into work in the morning,' said Mr Shipman.

NAMES FOR SMITHY JUNIOR

Billy Ricky - where he was conceived like the Beckhams

William Richard - posher version of where he was conceived. Classier

Rocky - No one would mess

Rambo - (See Rocky)

Trev - as in Brooking

Carlos - as in Tevez

~~Junior~~ - Peter Andre's bagged it

Gavin - could be seen as a bit gay though

Geoff - as in Hurst

Spike - Cool. But is it a dog's name?

Bobby - as in Moore

George - least Welsh name there is. means dragon slayer.

Di Canio - as in Paulo

Will - Will Smith! Fresh Prince! forget that. might get called big willy!

Smithy - Smithy Smith? Can you have too much Smith?

Neil Jnr. - after me

Dear Nessa,

What happened to you at the football on Saturday? One moment we were munching away on the canapés in the executive box. The next moment, you were gone. If your intention was to make me look like a numpty in front of my Dad; mission accomplished.

I've spent a fair bit of money trying to woo you and I'm going to be a bit annoyed if it's all been for no good. It wasn't easy to get you into the store after hours so you could shop there alone, not forgetting the 10% staff discount I sorted on anything you purchased. And Monaco yacht trips aren't cheap either. The yacht petrol alone is a small fortune. So if you've gone cool on me then that's just not on.

Look, I'm sorry if I'm sounding a bit narky. But the thing is, I really miss you, Nessa Jenkins. A few months back, I thought I'd done everything there was to do. Then I met you. Every time I close my eyes, all I see is you. I'll never regret getting that eyelid tattoo.

Nessa, we need to talk. So I'll call you on Saturday night after I'm back from the football. But remember, it's actually your turn to call me. I'll call you and let it ring twice, then hang up, then you call me back. It's only fair, money-wise.

All my love

Son of the Big Boss

PS - Just so you know, if you finish with me, I do have other options.
    You just wait and see.

ALRIGH',

FIRST OF ALL, I AM ENCLOSING £2.40, MY HALF OF THAT PAY AND DISPLAY TICKET WHICH YOU KEEP BANGING ON ABOUT. WE'RE EVENS NOW, SO BACK OFF.

NOW I WON'T LIE TO YOU, THE REASON I LEFT THE FOOTBALL EARLY WAS YOU BEIN' A TWAT. SIMPLE AS. THING IS, SEE, YOU WANT TO CHANGE ME. I'M NOT FOR THE CHANGING. I DON'T CARE IF YOUR OLD MAN RUNS A SHOP. THAT'S NO EXCUSE. I WENT OUT WITH A LAD CALLED GLYN WHOSE DAD WAS MANAGER OF CAERPHILLY MORRISONS AND HE NEVER MADE DEMANDS ON ME LIKE THAT. SO I THINK IT'S BEST IF YOU AND I JUST GET ON WITH OUR LIVES, 'COS I'M NOT CHANGIN' AND ULTIMATELY I DON'T SEE YOU CHANGIN' FROM BEIN' A TWAT.

IF YOU'RE STRUGGLIN' TO DEAL WITH THE SPLIT, MY ADVICE IS TO GO AWAY ON HOLIDAY FOR A BIT. BORROW THE YACHT. TAKE A BREAK. GET YOUR OLD MAN TO SORT YOU OUT WITH A REBOUND SHAG. THAT SHOULD HELP YOU MOVE ON. AND BEFORE WE GO OUR SEPARATE WAYS FOR GOOD, I HAVE ONE PIECE OF ADVICE WHICH MIGHT HELP YOU IN YOUR FUTURE RELATIONSHIPS. BIRDS DON'T LIKE IT WHEN YOU ASK THEM TO SPLIT THE COST OF A TEXT MESSAGE.

TIDY,

NESSA

PS. SORRY THE £2.40 IS IN COPPERS.

Barry Island Pleasure Park

Wales Premier Pleasure Park!

NAMES IDEAS FOR BABY JENKINS

NEIL - AFTER STACEY'S OLD BOSS. ALWAYS THOUGHT HE WAS A NICE GUY

DESHAWN? - BIT TOO R'N'B?

QUENTIN - SURE HE'LL GET BULLIED, BUT THAT WILL TOUGHEN HIM UP

SHAQUILLE - TOO BLACK?

NEIL - AFTER THE WELSH RUGBY LEGEND

FIDEL - MIGHT GET PRONOUNCED FIDDLE THOUGH.

DODI - ALWAYS LOVED IT, BUT PROBABLY NOT APPROPRIATE NOW...

ACHMED - LIKED THAT TOO. STACE WOULDN'T APPRECIATE IT THOUGH

HENSON - AFTER CHARLOTTE'S LOVELY LOOKING LAD

BARRY - AFTER THE ISLAND

SALMAN - FAVOURITE AUTHOR. BUT SOUNDS ODD WITH JENKINS

SISQO - TOO URBAN?

NEIL - AFTER DAD

Bryn!! What a super name!
Love Bryn.

NESSA'S

Knitting Patterns

I won't lie to you, knitting's not really my thing, even though it is one of the few sports you can do sitting down. But when you've got a bun in the oven and a few hours to kill, it can help to pass the time. And if, like me, you then get pregnant and lose all interest in baking, you'll have even more time on your hands.

All you need to get started are a pair of scissors, two knitting needles and some wool. Here's a tip: if you're passing through Barry, pick up a Chicken Noodlicious (no. 29) from Mystic Oriental Kebabs and Burgers on Wyndham Street and, not only will you get a decent-sized portion and two fresh-wipes to boot (useful for weekends away, girls), you'll get a free pair of chopsticks which, following a rinse, make cracking knitting needles. Unfortunately, it doesn't work the other way around: knitting needles just don't grip noodles.

So let's get to business. I'd recommend you start with something basic like a pullover. Using the scissors I mentioned earlier, snip one of the cuffs off and you'll find it unravels with ease, providing plenty of wool to start knitting with. I used one of Trevor's old pullovers which gave me wool in more colours than you could shake a (chop) stick at.

Once you've mastered the knit and purl (and I'm not being funny, but if you don't know what those are, you're better off going back to your baking) then you can start making something useful. And if you're looking for suggestions, I've got some suggestions. Three to be precise. And here they are. So get those chopsticks whirring.

1. BEGINNER - WELSH FLAG

It's a rectangle and it only has three colours, so you can't really go wrong. But if you do go wrong, my advice would be to make the dragon round, redo the bottom bit in white and turn it into the Japanese flag. Although this should be a last resort (unless you're Japanese). The flag looks cracking hanging in the cab of your truck.

2. INTERMEDIATE - BOWLING BALL BUFF

I know what you're thinking, you're thinking I've had a wobble and just put the same picture down. Well I haven't. Due to the mathematical impossibility of representing fairly and accurately a three-dimensional object on a two-dimensional page, you'd have no way of knowing that this time the flag does, in fact, sag a bit in the middle. That's so's it fits the curve of your bowling ball better and gives a more even, all-round shine post-buffing. Plus, it's bigger than the flag in section 1 so you'll need more wool. You could try another design if you like, but I'd really rather you didn't.

3. ADVANCED - HMS INVINCIBLE

This one's not for the faint-hearted, but then neither was going into battle aboard this lady of the sea. Brings back a lot of memories for me. I won't lie to you, I gets a little choked up thinking back – I only just made it back from the Falklands. I've knitted three of these now, to various scales, and I'm not going to hold your hand: by now you should know how to do it. You either got the ability or you don't. Simple as.

You'll need a crochet hook and a lot of grey wool.

BBC
DRAGONS' DEN

INTRODUCTION: Dear Peter Jones, Duncan Bannatyne, Simon Woodroffe/Theo Paphitis, Rachel Elnaugh/Deborah

Meaden, Doug Richard/Richard Farleigh/James Caan and Evan Davis.

It is very nice to meet you all. My sister-in-law, Gwen, has a business idea that's an absolute knock out. However, she's

quite a timid sort and was not keen on sending you her business proposal, but I told her : 'Nothing Ventured Nothing

Gained'. I eventually managed to coax her in to committing something to paper. So here is her proposal:

COMPANY NAME: Omlette Den

MANAGER: & Head Chef: Me (Gwen West)

ASSISTANT MANAGERS: & Accountant: Bryn West

DESCRIPTION: Well what I was thinking was, me and
Bryn could start up an omelette restaurant. It would be
a bit like a KFC, but for omelettes.
We would do two different styles of Omelette:
EAT IN: Omelette on a plate. /
TAKE AWAY: Omelette rolled up and put in a napkin.
I would make a selection of five omelettes (cheese, ham,
ham & cheese, tomato & ham and tomato) and if you ask
for an Omelette Meal you would get a cup of tea with it.
I'm not sure if this is a good idea, but I haven't seen an omelette
restaurant before. So there's a definite gap in the market. I asked three of my
friends and they all thought it was an excellent idea - so that's something isn't it?
Our current business plan is that we would start with a small shop, then get a
bigger shop then get more shops. Very much like Starbucks.
Omelettes are also cheap, which must be a good thing mustn't it?

DEAL: I have a few hundred quid saved up, so I could put that in. Then you could have, say, 50% of the business for however much you can afford. What you investors think is a small amount of money is actually quite a lot of money to me. So I'd be happy with whatever you can give me.

FURTHER INFORMATION: As you can see, Gwen's proposal is a very good one. If that doesn't convince you, all that we ask is that you invite us on to your TV show and let Gwen cook you one. I promise that once you've tasted it you would not be able to say no.

We very much look forward to being on your programme.

I will ask you one thing, mind. Gwen has been through a tough time after her husband Trevor (God rest his soul) died. I have seen your show and I know that you can be very rude. So I ask you — please be polite to her. She is a lovely lady and I'm sure you'll all get on with her.

Many thanks,

Bryn (on behalf of Gwen)

Gwen's

Book Reviews

★★★☆☆

Please Mummy, No (One Man's Struggle To Break The Cycle)
By Peter Lacey

I have to say, it wasn't the most fun book I've ever read. The most fun book I've ever read was probably a Ben Elton one. Actually, I didn't even choose this book. I joined one of those book clubs from the adverts in the TV magazine and then if one month you don't buy a book, they send you one anyway. And you have to pay for it. I tried to get out of it - I've written dozens of letters, but they won't back down. It's been a real ordeal, I can tell you. Though obviously not as much of an ordeal as this author's gone through.

Was this review helpful to you?

★★☆☆☆

No Daddy, Please Don't (One Man's Struggle To Break The Cycle)
By Peter Lacey

Like the first book in this series, this one's also pretty heavy going. It also really makes you think. It mainly made me think that I should order something from the book club next month rather than let them send me another one of their choice. Without meaning to diminish the terrible time the author has had, when you've read one of these books, you've pretty much read them all. Perhaps instead of wallowing in self pity for a second time, the author could have spent some of the money he got from the first book by doing something to take his mind off it all. Like bowling, go-karting or bingo.

Was this review helpful to you?

Guinness Book Of Records (2002)

Well I've been very busy recently and that's probably why I forgot to order a book again. I'm guessing that 2002 wasn't a great year for record breaking and that's why they had so many left over and sent me this last month. Anyway, there are a few interesting facts from 2002, though I suppose they might be out of date by now. One I liked was the biggest kite in the world. 30 foot wide! And also the tallest mountain is still Mount Everest.

Was this review helpful to you?

A Collection Of Banksy's Artwork

Okay, so I did deliberately order this one. But I thought it was art done by Jeff Banks who used to do the Clothes Show. I assumed that he must have stopped doing fashion and done a bit of painting or sculpture instead. He always did look like the creative sort, like my Jason. Turns out I was wrong and actually this is just a book of graffiti that a vandal has done. I feel ashamed that I have helped him profit from his antisocial behaviour. There's no picture of him on the inside cover – which is odd. But perhaps the police can write to the book publishers to get his address, then they can arrest him.

Was this review helpful to you?

Don't Auntie, Don't
(One Man's Struggle To Break The Cycle)
By Peter Lacey

For Pete's sake man, get over yourself.

Was this review helpful to you?

facebook

home   account   privacy   logout

Profile edit   **Friends** ▼   **Inbox** ▼

Search

Applications edit

- Photos
- Applications
- Marketplace
- Events
- Superprod!
- Likeness
- Friends GPS

Share you photos with
friends on Facebook

Gwen West

is letting Bryn set-up her facebook page.

Updated on Monday edit

View photos of Gwen (1)

View Gwen Friends (1)

Prod Gwen

Throw a sheep at Gwen

Networks:	Wales
Sex:	Female
Relationship status	Married **to** Trevor West
Hometown:	Barry Island

▼ **Information**

Interests:	Cooking fantastic omelettes, barn dancing, a good old natter with the neighbours.
Favourite Music:	Suzi Quatro, James Blunt (I introduced her to it. And she did say she liked it – Bryn), Donny Osmond.
Favourite TV Shows:	I like cookery programs although I don't like that man who swears. I think he should just cook more.
Favourite Movies:	Gone with the Wind (although, again, it would be better without the swearing). Sense and Sensibility (because of the hunky, polite men)
Favourite Books:	Gwen is still trying to think of her favourite book so for now I'm going to put Gone with the Wind, Sense and Sensibility.
Favourite Quotes:	'Gwen I really do think you are marvelous.' Trevor (not his exact words, I paraphrase – Bryn)

▼ **Friends**

1 friends   See all

Bryn

▼ **Photos**

0 albums   See all

▼ **Mini-Feed**

0 stories   Import | See all

▼ **The Wall**

Displaying 1 of 1 wallposts   Import | See all

Write something on your own wall...

Bryn West (Barry) wrote at 11.32pm

Hello Gwen. By all means reply to this message. But do be aware that other people may be able to see and read it. So if you want to send a private message it's best to send an e-mail. Or give me a call and I'll pop round.

Wall-to-Wall - Write on (name) wall - Delete

BRYN & NESSA'S DUET SHORTLIST FOR GWEN'S SURPRISE BIRTHDAY

Okay, Nessa, so I've narrowed it down to eight possibilities. But, truth be told, I'm struggling to narrow it down any further. I've looked at the pros and the cons and, quite simply, it's too close to call. So please have a look through and let me know which ones you prefer. Then we can create a short-shortlist. From there we can narrow it down to a final two, then we'll make the ultimate selection. If you want, you could always text me your selections to make it feel a bit like X Factor!

THE GIRL IS MINE (Michael Jackson & Paul McCartney)
Pros: It's by the two greatest songsmiths ever to grace this planet. Therefore on paper, it's the greatest song ever written!

Cons: The lyrics might make it sound like we're fighting over a girl. Which could appear a bit peculiar and certainly won't be any kind of tribute to Gwen on her birthday.

SOMETHING STUPID (Frank Sinatra & Nancy Sinatra)
Pros: We know it backwards! Well, not literally backwards. Though if we did, perhaps we could go on Britain's Got Talent next year as backwards song-singers!

Cons: I'm no Robbie Williams or Frank Sinatra. They're both cracking-looking fellas and I'm concerned that comparisons from the party guests will be inevitable.

CRAZY IN LOVE (Beyonce & Jay-Z)
Pros: It's a very jolly song so it's bound to get people dancing, even the youngsters.

Con: I'm really struggling to learn Jaz-Y's melody. It's quite monotone and that makes it difficult to pick out the notes. Also I'm not good with a New York accent – it comes out sounding South African. And perhaps the final nail in the coffin is it's not the easiest song to line dance to.

NOTHING'S GONNA STOP US NOW (Starship)
Pros: Out of all these songs, it's probably this one which best utilises my rock voice capabilities.

Cons: It always makes me think of that film Mannequin when a man has relations with a shop doll. Not exactly family viewing is it? So perhaps it's not suitable for a family party.

AIN'T NO MOUNTAIN HIGH ENOUGH (Marvin Gaye & Tammi Terrell)

Pros: What a belter! All that singing about mountains and valleys, I'd always assumed these two were Welsh! I looked it up on Wikipedia and it turns out that a) they're both American and b) he was shot by his Dad. That certainly wouldn't have happened if he had been Welsh.

Cons: While I am by no means the weakest singer in the Barry Male Voice Choir, I must confess that keeping up with all the wibbly-wobbly stuff that Marvin Gaye does begs some pretty big questions of me. Questions which I'm not sure I can answer, either.

HAPPY BIRTHDAY (Stevie Wonder)

Pros: Perfect for a birthday celebration! It's almost as if Stevie wrote it with that in mind.

Cons: Put simply, it's not a duet.

ISLANDS IN THE STREAM (Kenny Rogers & Dolly Parton)

Pros: It was always Trevor's favourite song (God rest his soul), so I'm sure Gwen would very much appreciate the gesture.

Cons: I do have that nasty habit of slipping into 'Ghetto Superstar' on the chorus, don't I? I'm sorry! But that version just happens to be one of the catchiest songs of 1999.

GHETTO SUPERSTAR (That Is What You Are) (Pras Michael featuring Mya)

Pros: I suppose I'm only including this as a kind of Islands In The Stream failsafe.

Cons: Probably not what Trevor would have wanted. Or what Gwen will want.

Bryn's

Line Dancing Steps Guide (Islands In The Stream)

Dear Friend of Gwen,

You all need to be ready for Gwen's surprize party. We will be doing a line dance there, and you will need to learn it. So I've found a copy of some steps on the internet for you to swot up on.

Remember, this is a surprize party — if you let our Gwen know anything about it, with God as my witness, I will kill you. Also don't be late! I don't want her getting wind of it. Is that completely clear?

Bryn

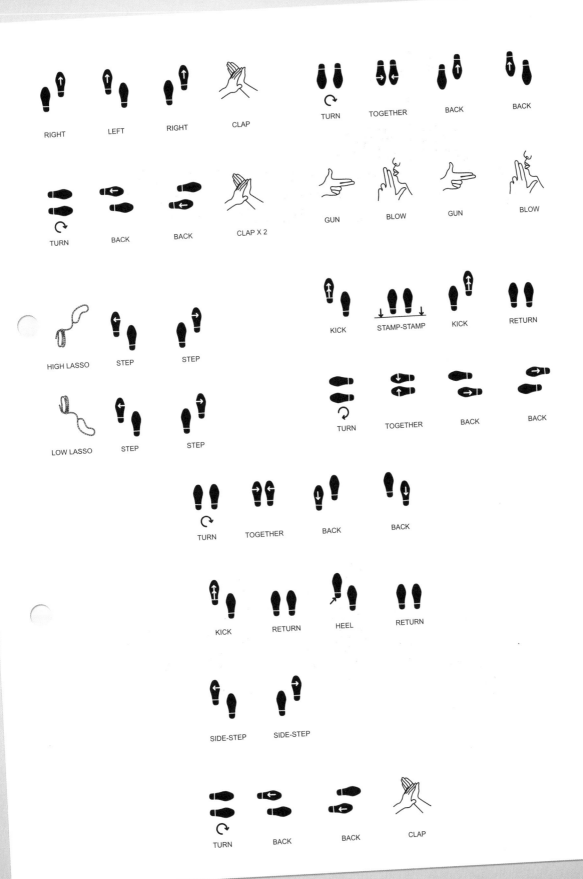

THE GREAT ALEXO

SECRETS OF MAGIC

Alright. I'm 'The Great Alex-o'. I do magic for events. Weddings, birthday parties ... that's it. So you want to know how to do magic? Fine. I can do tricks like sawing a man in half. Or sawing a woman in half. Or sawing an old man in half. Or sawing an old woman in half.

I don't know how to saw a kid in half. So don't ask me to do that. I wouldn't want to anyway.

CARD TRICKS

Want to know a card trick? Fine. Ask whoever to pick a card. Put it on the top of the pack. Or bottom. Wherever. Doesn't matter. Shuffle it. Badly. Take the card off the top or wherever. It'll still be there. 'Cos you shuffled it badly. It's not magic or anything.

SWORD CABINET

Putting swords through a woman. Put the woman in box. Tell woman in box to avoid the swords. Then shove 'em in. That's it. Just a girl bending round swords. What did you think it was? Mystical stuff? Well it's not. Mystical stuff's a bunch of crap. Doesn't exist. It can't.

SAWING A WOMAN IN HALF

Want to saw a kid in half? Told you before. Can't be done. Wouldn't do it anyway. Quit asking. Want to know how to saw a man/woman/old man/old woman in half? Everyone does. Anyway it's dead simple: It's not their legs, is it? It couldn't be, 'cos you can't saw an actual man and woman in half with them getting hurt. Think it through. It's a midget's legs. Has to be.

RABBIT IN THE HAT

Two words: 'Rabbit compartment'

So there we go. It's all lies. There's no such thing as magic.

If you would like to hire The Great Alex-o call (07700) 900221.
Don't worry if he doesn't pick up. He screens his calls.

 Pam's

Fencing Tips

Dear New Starter,

Hello, I'm Pam! If you are reading this, that means that you have now joined Billericay Women's Fencing for the Over 40s. Welcome! You have probably already met Susan (the 'curvy' lady who runs the group). Well Susan asked me to put together a little document for new starters so you can get to grips with the basics. That's what this is!

Firstly, I should congratulate you on choosing such an excellent sport. Fencing not only develops your co-ordination, it also helps you to develop sword-fighting skills, which other non sword-based activities do not.

Below you will find all the details you should need to get started. I look forward to fighting you soon!

Best wishes,

Pamela Shipman

Billericay Women's Fencing For The
Over 40s Social Secretary

BILLERICAY WOMEN'S FENCING FOR THE OVER 40s

* Are you interested in taking up fencing?
* Are you a woman?
* Are you over 40?
* Are you from the Billericay Area?
* Are you clear of any heart impediments?
* Are you free on Thursday mornings 9am-10am?

If you answered 'Yes' to these six questions, then Billericay Women's Fencing For The Over 40s might possibly be for you. For more information email bigfatsue55@hotmail.com.

Meet the Team

PAMELA SHIPMAN (SOCIAL SECRETARY)

Pamela, a founder member of the club, is our wonderful social secretary.

Pam is Essex born and bred and lives in Billericay with her husband Mick and son Gavin. Pam recently became a mother-in-law when Gavin married his Welsh girlfriend Stacey. The wedding was a very classy affair which, and I know Pam's going to be mortified that I said this, was paid for by Mick and Pam and not the bride's family. Sorry Pam, but your unselfishness shouldn't mean you get no credit!

Pam knows anyone who's anyone in Billericay which makes her the perfect social secretary. It was Pam who organized our fantastic club trip to Bluewater in a minibus, a trip which included us seeing Linda Lusardi in H&M. Pam also pulled off quite a coup by getting us girls tickets to the filming of A Question of Sport. The one we watched had Dwain Chambers and Frankie Dettori on – it was hilarious! Next month Pam is aiming us to get tickets to a filming of The Weakest Link: Celebrity Addicts Special.

Pam also does a lot of charity work (which I'm sure she'd rather I didn't mention) including work for 'The Badgers Trust', 'Say No To The Mast' and 'Cure Dog Measles'.

PAM'S FAVOURITES
- Meal: Vegetarian Steak.
- Pin Up: My Mick
- Role Model: Camilla Parker-Bowles
- TV Show: Pet Rescue
- Last Txt Message You Received:
  "Will be in an all afternoon meeting with Chalky and Woodruff. Mick."

Pam's Christmas Card List - 2007

Bryn + Gwen
(Invite for Christmas Day. Say there'll be turkey AND nut roast in case they turn vegetarian in the mean time)

Japanese Margaret + Japanese Takeshi
(Check whether they celebrate Christmas first)

Non-Japanese Margaret + family
(Definitely celebrates Christmas)

Dawn + Pete
(Ask if Pete will bring some of those sausages over for Boxing Day tea)

Seth
(Check postal costs to Ghana. Maybe send him some tinned food and one of Mick's old jumpers too)

Cath (+ Smithy, Rudi)
(Remember not to muff up seasonal message by alluding to Cath's lesbian fling)

No Man Jan
(Address it to her new fella too ? Stan ?)

Fat No More Pat + Fatter Chris
(Don't congratulate Pat on weight loss - it will just make Chris feel sad)

Fingers, Dirtbox, Chinese Alan, Budgie, Gary, Simon, Swede, Deano, Jesus
(No need for a card. Just send a cheeky group text. Get Gav to show me how)

Picky Vicky
(Ask how her allergies are)

Homosexual Lionel
(Check whether they celebrate Christmas first)

Capriccios
(Try and send one before their printed card arrives)

Big Fat Sue + Big Fat Kev
(Do not invite for Boxing Day this year. Never enough leftovers)

Smokey Brian + Liz
(Wish Brian all the best for his chemo)

Rita + Non-Japanese Takeshi
(Send early - they'll be in Korea for Christmas)

Karen the Hippy
(Send an email card. Otherwise she'll have another maggie about me wasting paper)

Bevvy Bev
(Ask how her bowels are doing)

Betty + Reg
(Be sensitive. Could be either of their last Christmases)

The Prince Of Wales and The Duchess Of Cornwall
(Don't use a card from the charity box for Charles and Camilla. Buy a five pound one from Paperchase)

Smithy's and Gavin's

Drinking Games

DRINKALONGA SOUND OF MUSIC

Down a shot when you see the Baroness. Get a tinny and drink when you see a Nazi. Down it when the Captain kisses Maria. Remember though that you still have to sing along with the songs ... which you'll be doing anyway by half way in.

SWEAR WORD A-Z

An updated classic. Go round the table naming a swearword beginning with each letter of the alphabet. But as per usual, you have to drink while you think. Down the pint if you want to pass. Here's a few useful words : Quim, Xixi (Portuguese), Yang Pipe, Zoosexual. If you don't know what they mean, look them up.

1-2-3 DRINK

This is the simplest game. Pick a leader. The leader then counts to three. Then you drink. Excellent game if you're pressed for time.

FORTUNE DRINKING

Get yourself a pack of Tarot cards. Deal yourself four cards. Drink for each card. Royalty means you have to down a shot. Sun/Moon/Stars, down a half pint. Death and you down both. Plus you find out a bit about your future at the same time.

THE Y WORD

Watch any programme involving Gordon Ramsey. Drink two fingers when he says 'Yes'. Drink four fingers whenever you hear a bleep. No one's ever made it past the first ad break.

HIDE AND DRINK

One guy counts to 20 and everyone has to hide around the house (or, even better, pub). He then has to leave his post to try and find the others. If he can tag them before they get to the post then they have to down their pints. If he doesn't, and they beat him to the post then he has to down his pint.

HEAT MAGAZINE SPOTTED

Pass round a copy of Heat magazine, turning the page every time it gets to you. Down two fingers if you see a Big Brother Contestant. Three fingers if you see fashion faux pas. Four fingers if you see Sarah Jessica Parker. Whoever gets the 'Spotted' has to down their pint. If you land on the 'Circle of Shame' page, you have to do the rest of your drinking with your trousers round your ankles.

DRINK MURDER

Very similar to wink murder. One person is picked as the detective. They have to leave the room. Then pick the drink murderer. The detective then returns and has to work out who the murderer is. Every time the murderer winks at you you have to drink. Once your drink is gone, you're dead. If the murderer is rumbled they have to down their pint. The detective has one chance to pick the murderer – if they get it wrong, they have to down their pint.

DRINK KNOCK OUT

Similar to 1-2-3 Drink but without the counting. You line up your drinks and down them one by one. The first one to pass out wins. Though you'll have to wait till they come round before you can tell them they won.

BONUS GAME: DRINK CHICKEN

This is only for extreme drinkers. Play any of the above games from above, but every pint you down has to belong to someone else in the pub.

Smithy's **Pub Quiz**

Questions

Q1 -   Which former England football
       international joined Japanese
       team Nagoya Grampus Eight in 1993?

Q2 -   According to "Beers Of The World"
       magazine's poll, which is
       the best ale in the world?

Q3 -   Which historically significant event
       occurred in London on the 4th April 1994?

Q4 -   What was New Order's only
       UK Number 1 single?

Q5 -   Who won the ice dancing at the
       Winter Olympics in the 80s?

Q6 -   Who won FHM's
       fittest bird in 2006?

Q7 -   Who won the golden boot, Mexico '86?

Q8 -   Who took over from Des Lynam
       on BBC1's Match Of The Day?

Q9 -   Which town do Fray Bentos
       pies originate from?

Q10 - Who invented 'the robot'?

Q11 - Which Top Ten hit, released in February 2000, celebrated a particular item of women's underwear?

Q12 - Who won the Olympics in 2005?

Q13 - Which Midlands city, the second biggest in the UK, home of the NEC and Aston Villa, has more miles of canal than Venice?

Q14 - How old was Hayden Panettiere when she first appeared in the sci-fi series 'Heroes'?

Q15 - What is the only animal that begins with the letter 'G'?

I am a woman.
My husband likes to
dress me as a schoolboy
which keeps our marriage
FANDABIDOZI. Who am I?

Q16 - How many times has the entertainer Darren Day been engaged?

Q17 - I am a woman. My husband likes me to dress as a schoolboy which keeps our marriage fandabidozi. Who am I?

Q18 - Who did the best version of Bohemian Rhapsody?

Q19 - The town of Leicester is the birthplace of which mass murderer?

Q21 - Pascal Chimbonda moved to Tottenham for what transfer fee?

Q22 - Gary Lineker moved from Everton to Barcelona for what transfer fee?

Q23 - Gary Lineker moved from Barcelona to Tottenham for what transfer fee?

Q24 - Which great sportsman does the Walkers crisps adverts?

Q25 - Who done the voice of "Underground Ernie"?

Q26 - Where are 'French fries' originally from?

Q27 - Can badgers cry?

Q28 - Which French fullback did Tottenham sign off Wigan for £4.5m?

Q29 - Who invented the plug?

- -

TIE BREAK QUESTION
What is the highest number of goals scored by an England international footballer?

- -

1ST PLACE PRIZE: TWO PACKETS OF HAMLET

2ND PLACE PRIZE: A PACKET OF HAMLET

3RD PLACE PRIZE: A SINGLE HAMLET PANATELLA

ANSWERS

Q1 -   Gary Lineker.

Q2 -   Harviestoun Bitter & Twisted 4.2%.

Q3 -   West Ham beat Spurs 4-1 at White Hart Lane
        (Marsh, Morley, Morley, Steve Jones).

Q4 -   'World In Motion'.

Q5 -   Torvill & Dean.

Q6 -   Scarlett Johansson.

Q7 -   Gary Lineker.

Q8 -   Gary Lineker.

Q9 -   The town of Fray Bentos in Uruguay.

Q10 -   Josef Capek. But just for the record, the
        dance "The Robot" was invented by Smithy.

Q11 -   Sisqo's The Thong Song.

Q12 -   Lord Sebastian Coe won it. That's why
        the 2012 Olympics are in London.

Q13 -   Birmingham. Amazing, isn't it?
        Statistically better than Venice.

Q14 -   She was 17. Young, but she seems quite mature.
        That guy she goes out with from Heroes is 12
        years older than her. And no one goes on about
        her being too young for him, do they?

Q15 -   You could have had 'Giraffe' or 'Gorilla'.

Q16 -   6 times. The latest one must be a right mug.

Q17 -   I am Janette Krankie.

Q18 - G4.

Q19 - Apologies. The question was meant to be "The town of
        Leicester is birthplace of which television
        fashion consultant of Anglo-Chinese heritage?"
        And the answer was meant to be Gok Wan. But
        anyone who put Gok Wan will still get a point.

Q21 - £4.5m.

Q22 - £2.2m.

Q23 - £1.2m.

Q24 - Gary Lineker.

Q25 - Gary Lineker.

Q26 - Belgium.

Q27 - Yes. I saw it on Pet Rescue. Broke my heart.

Q28 - Pascal Chimbonda.

Q29 - Harvey Hubbell II.

Q30 - Kris Akabusi.

TIE BREAK QUESTION - 50 ODD, SCORED BY GARY LINEKER

THE WINNING TEAMS
1st Place Prize: BILLERICAY BRAINBOXES
2nd Place Prize: PAMELA-AND-HER-SON
            (AND HUSBAND) AND FRIENDS)
3rd Place Prize: MASSIVE SHANKERS

Smithy's Cruise, Marry, Shag Quiz

For the Boys

Kate Moss   Paris Hilton   Jordan

Sharon Osborne, Anne Robinson, Little Jimmy Krankie

Marie Curie, Florence Nightingale, Carol Vorderman

Billie Piper, Catherine Tate, Freema Agyeman

Delia Smith, Nigella Lawson, Supernanny

The Queen, Princess Anne, Duchess of York

Jessica Rabbit, Betty Boop, Velma from Scooby Doo

Posh Spice, Baby Spice, Ginger Spice

Britney Spears, Christina Aguilera, Madonna

Pete Burns, Jade Goody, Jackie Stallone

Cruise, Marry, Shag should be played with friends or, even better, family. The more awkward the game is the better. So don't wimp out – get Gran involved.

Okay, so here's the rules. I'm going to give you three people. One of them you have to marry, and have kids with and a dog and a family estate car and all that, you know, forever. One you have to go on a cruise ship around the world with, spending every minute of every day with them – but you do not have to sleep with them. And the other one you have to have a long, hard, brutal shag with.

For the Girls

James Blunt   Simon Cowell   Jamie Oliver

Bernard Manning, Lloyd Grossman, Frank Bruno

Elijah Wood, Orlando Bloom, Ian McKellen

David Tennant, Christopher Eccleston, Tom Baker

George Clooney, Wayne Rooney, DJ Spooney

Steve Tyler - Aerosmith, Brian May - Queen, Rick Parfitt - Status Quo

David Hasslehoff, BA Baracus, Sylvester Stallone

Stephen Hawking, Albert Einstein, Stephen Fry

Jeremy Clarkson, James May, Richard Hammond

Barry Chuckle, Christopher Biggins, Michael Winner

facebook | **Profile** edit | **Friends** ▾ | **Inbox** ▾ | home | account | privacy | logout

Search

Applications edit

- Photos
- Applications
- Marketplace
- Events
- Superprod!
- Likeness
- Friends GPS

Share you photos with friends on Facebook

View photos of Rudi (156)

View Rudi's Friends (3,267)

Prod Rudi

Give a WKD to Rudi

Rudi Smith

is da original Smithy – not my brother, me!!!!!!!!!!!!!

Updated on Monday edit

Network:	Essex
Sex:	Female
Relationship Status:	Single. Deffo not with Darren Millar
Hometown:	Billericay

▾ Information

Interests:	WKD Blue. WKD Orange. WKD Red.
Favourite Music:	Dizzee Rascal. Lethal Bizzle. Sway. Basically anything off BassFace FM (Billericay's #1 Pirate Radio Station)
Favourite TV Shows:	TV's for old age bastards. I only watch youtube. But on youtube I watch Eastenders, Casualty and Supernanny.
Favourite Movies:	American Pie. American Pie 2. American Wedding. American Pie Presents: Band Camp. American Pie Presents: The Naked Mile. American Pie: Beta House. American History X (which wasn't as funny as the first 6)
Favourite Books:	*Jade: My Autobiography* (OMG, she has been through so much. Amazing story. Plus three people I know get a mention.)
Favourite Quotes:	'You can't judge me' Rudi Smith 'The quality of mercy is not strain'd, It droppeth as the gentle rain from heaven Upon the place beneath.' For more intellectual quotes text QUOTE to 81123

▾ Friends

3,267 friends See all

Gavin

Shanice

Cherice

▸ Mini-Feed

Displaying 4 stories Import | See all

Today

Rudi wrote on Cherice Davis' **wall** at 12.01pm

The day before Yesterday

Rudi Bitch-slapped Cherice Davis at 11.55am

The day before Yesterday

Rudi Drop-kicked Cherice Davis at 11.53am

▾ Photos

1 of 52 albums See all

Burberry

Billericay Burnout

The Wall

Displaying **5 of 104** wallposts   Import | See all

Write something on your own wall...

Post

Dave Clark (Billericay) wrote at 11.32pm

Hey, heard you ran into Cherice. I can't believe her aunty! Sly, man. Sly.

Cherice Davis (Billericay) wrote at 3.24pm

Stay away from Darren. Stop pokin' and textin' him. Remember, I told you.

Neil Smith (Billericay) wrote at 11.32pm

I wish I was a little bit taller,
I wish I was a baller,
I wish I had a girl who would dream that I would call her!
Modern classic!

Cherice Davis (Billericay) wrote at 9.38am on June 1st, 2007

Are you stupid or somfin'? I just seen your number come up on Darren's phone. You better pray I don't see you out tonight!

▼ **Groups**   ✕

4 groups   See all

BassFace FM is da Bomb • Join This Group If You Reckon Cherice Davis Has Noshed Over 100 Guyz • Everyone I Ever Met Called Shanice Woz a Prossie • Billericay Threshers Appreciation Society

▼ **Gifts**   ✕

You have 1 gifts   Send a Gift

From Bryn

Smithy's

Handshake

STEP 1 - PARTNER SELECTION

Make your selection carefully. They will need to be agile, dexterous and have the smarts required for such a complex routine.

STEP 2 - RAPPER'S GRIP

Once your shake partner has been chosen, start with a classic right-handed gangster 90 degree grip.

STEP 3 - CLASSIC FINGER HOOK

Bend your fingers in unison to form a hook shape. Lock your hook with your partner's (monkey grip). That's the finger lock.

STEP 4 - THE TOUCH

Clench your right fist. Touch it against your partner's.

STEP 5 - O.P.T.P

It's straight out of The Touch into a classic 'One Potato, Two Potato'.

STEP 6 - DOUBLE SIDEWAYS SLAP

Slap sideways once. Then come back, back-hand slapping as you go.

STEP 7 - ELBOW PIZAZZ

Time to bring in the left arm. Raise your left elbow and tap it against your partner's.

STEP 8 - THE PAT-A-CAKE

Don't be fooled into thinking this move is just child's play. After seven gruelling handshake steps, this is no picnic. Focus hard. You're nearly there.

STEP 9 - FIST RETREAT

Clench both fists and retract them into their respective shoulders.

STEP 10 - THE DOUBLE TOUCH

Release both fists. Touch knuckles with your partner.

STEP 11 - CHEST SLAM

Jump up and forwards, colliding your chest with your partners.

STEP 12 - THE SWAGGER

Handshake complete. All that's left to do is soak up the admiring glances. Swagger away.

Smithy's and Gavin's

ENGLAND XI

PETER SHILTON
Gav: Somewhat controversial – Smithy was lobbying for Gordon Banks but I don't think you can argue with Shilts. The man was a rock.

VIV ANDERSON
Smithy: Right back has been our toughest position to fill. Mick Mills, Gary Neville and Alf Ramsey were all in contention. Until one day Gav comes into the Crown with his arms held aloft and shouts 'Big Viv Anderson!' Everyone in the pub agreed – this man fits the make up of this team brilliantly.

RIO
Smithy: Without question Rio has to be in. The man has the lot. The most graceful centre back in the world. A born leader, a natural finisher and looks like a top bloke who loves a few pints down his local. I live for the day he's back in a West Ham shirt. The king and captain of our team.

SIR BOBBY MOORE
Gav: We both agree on this one. Quite simply the finest player of his generation. World Cup winner and the only one who has made our team.

JULIAN DICKS
Smithy: Gav says it is a joke to put Dicksy in an England shirt, and to some extent I agree. As both a footballer and a golfer the man is a joke. But it's for that reason he has to be in the team. Hard as you like and a true Upton Park legend.

BECKS
Gav: The man, the myth, the god, the girth. Forget Posh Spice and the tattoos. And all the celebrity stuff. Remember the guy scoring from the half way line. Last minute free kicks against Greece. Refusing to mug off Steve McLaren even though he should have done. He is the man and you know it!

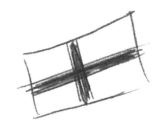

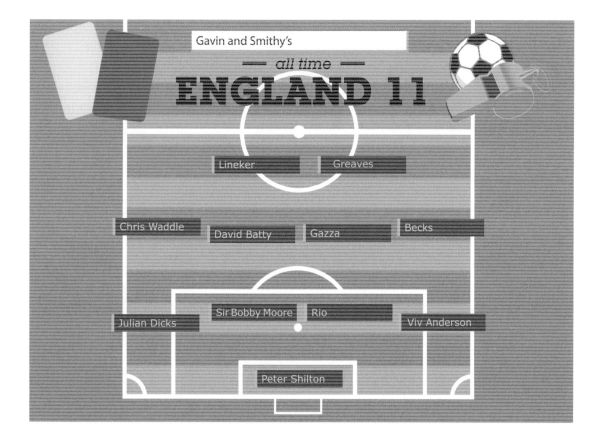

Gavin and Smithy's
all time
ENGLAND 11

Lineker   Greaves

Chris Waddle   David Batty   Gazza   Becks

Sir Bobby Moore   Rio
Julian Dicks   Viv Anderson

Peter Shilton

DAVID BATTY

Gav: Now Smithy and I disliked Leeds as much as everyone else when they were buying everyone and being good. But we always had a soft spot for this little mentalist! Hard as it gets and the perfect foil for Gazza. I wanted Paul Ince but Smithy said he'd remove his name from the above if Judas made our team. So Batty it is.

GAZZA

Smithy: I love him, just like you do and just like your mum does. Italia '90, officially the best World Cup of my lifetime and here's the star man! His vision, his passion and his dentist chair celebrations all make this guy the best our country has. Without him there'd be no Joe Cole. Think about it…

CHRIS WADDLE

Gav: A no-brainer for me. Forget the songs, forget the hair, forget the terrible clothes and just close your eyes and see the man skipping past defenders and spraying pinpoint passes around the place, not to mention the odd screamer here and there. A god!

LINEKER/GREAVES

Now we tried to pick a pairing that would work well together and personally I can't believe Sir Trevor Brooking ain't in our team. But Gav is right – imagine the post-match punditry these two would offer! Amazing.

REAL READERS' STORIES

HOT AND BUTTERY

'Aren't you going to come in?' Asked Kitty. She beckoned the plumber in to the bedroom. Her bed sheets fell slightly, exposing one of her corn on the cobs.

'Are you feeling hot?' she asked.

'Yes. That could be a problem with the boiler. I'm guessing that the diverter valve isn't turning off properly. It'll take a few days to order in the parts.'

'Well how about you take off some clothes to cool yourself down.'

'Yeah, but that would only be a temporary fix. I'd have to charge you double call-out and I wouldn't want to do that to a sexy housewife like you. I could check if there's any air in the system, that could be causing the valve to ...' Kitty grabbed the plumber and pulled him towards her. He accidentally ran his hands over her buttery corn on the cobs.

> My flatmate Sapphire is going to be back in a bit. She could join us for a spicy sandwich.

'I want you to corn on the cob me.' she screamed. 'I want you to corn on the cob me till we can't do it anymore!'

'Don't worry. I've got enough corn on the cob to last us the whole night. I went large.' Kitty ran her hand over his chicken nuggets and started to release the pressure on his free 1.5L bottle of coke.

'Shall I put my nuggets in your family bucket?' he enquired. She nodded seductively. Then he slowly reached over and grabbed her buns.

'I don't mind you having a piece of my saucy zinger, as long as you let me nosh on your corn on the cob. Just mind you don't get sticky fingers.' She moaned.

'I've just lost one of my nuggets in your family bucket. I'll try and retrieve it, but I'm going to have to go in quite deep.'

'That's okay with me.'

Kitty looked the plumber directly in the eye.

'My flatmate Sapphire is going to be back in a bit. She could join us for a spicy sandwich.' The plumber looked uneasy.

'I'm not sure there'll be enough to go around,' he said.

Just then the bedroom door burst open. It was Sapphire, clutching her own bucket.

'Hey guys, who wants a taste of my Viennetta?'

Then things got really messy ... but that story will have to wait until next month.

This story was sent in by Anonymous of Billericay

Essex | change location   post an ad   manage my ads   help ?

Essex > Personals > Casual encounters > **Couples seeking men**

Couples seeking men

Je ne sais pas pourquoi

Date: Thursday 24th June

Location: Essex

WE ARE:

A beautiful, young, sexy girl and a short chartered surveyor looking for a third party to inject some 'Je ne sais pas pourquoi' into the bedroom.

YOU ARE:

From Ivory Coast, Burkina Faso, Ghana, Nigeria, Cameroon or similar area. Ideally you like basketball and have a good sense of rhythm. Non-Caucasian.

DETAILS

We are happy to act out scenarios and have the following costumes: Pilot, Sailor, Naughty Nurse and Cobbler. Feel free to provide your own. All expenses will be covered. (In the case of Dogging, all petrol to and from the car park will be paid. Please keep Pay & Display ticket for full reimbursement.)

If you are interested, or if you want a full list of our 'boundaries' and 'safewords', please e-mail dawn@xxxhotpersonals.com

Je ne sais pas pourquoi   posting ref: 123SEXI

Search

Bryn's

Gadget Guide

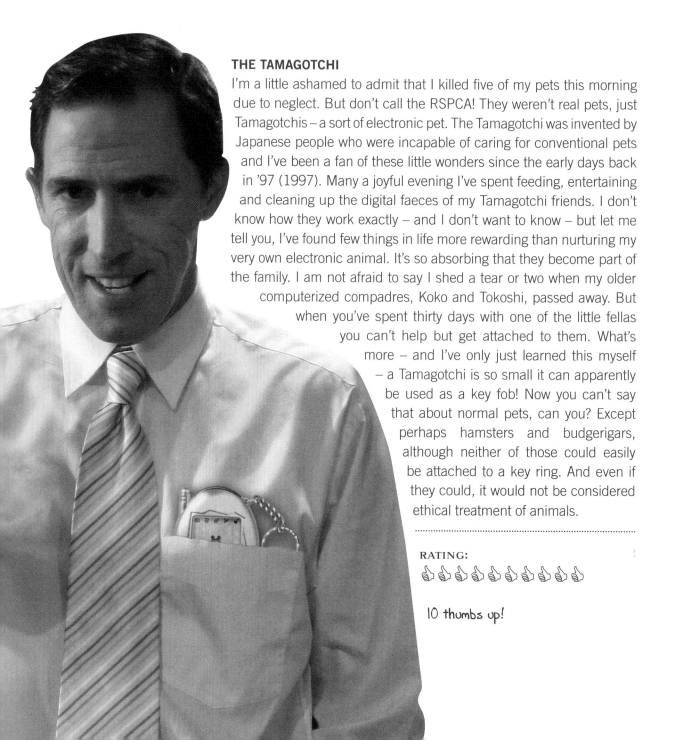

THE TAMAGOTCHI

I'm a little ashamed to admit that I killed five of my pets this morning due to neglect. But don't call the RSPCA! They weren't real pets, just Tamagotchis – a sort of electronic pet. The Tamagotchi was invented by Japanese people who were incapable of caring for conventional pets and I've been a fan of these little wonders since the early days back in '97 (1997). Many a joyful evening I've spent feeding, entertaining and cleaning up the digital faeces of my Tamagotchi friends. I don't know how they work exactly – and I don't want to know – but let me tell you, I've found few things in life more rewarding than nurturing my very own electronic animal. It's so absorbing that they become part of the family. I am not afraid to say I shed a tear or two when my older computerized compadres, Koko and Tokoshi, passed away. But when you've spent thirty days with one of the little fellas you can't help but get attached to them. What's more – and I've only just learned this myself – a Tamagotchi is so small it can apparently be used as a key fob! Now you can't say that about normal pets, can you? Except perhaps hamsters and budgerigars, although neither of those could easily be attached to a key ring. And even if they could, it would not be considered ethical treatment of animals.

RATING:
👍👍👍👍👍👍👍👍👍👍

10 thumbs up!

THE PHOTO PRINTER

'A printer?' I hear you say, 'A printer? What is so exciting about a printer?' Well, I'll tell you what. This one doesn't just print boring old documents. No, it prints colour photographs. Honest to God! Actual photo-quality photos. It's literally as simple as taking a pic (picture) on your digital camera, connecting the camera to a computer, loading the enclosed software on the computer, downloading the picture to the computer, cropping the picture on the computer, saving the picture on

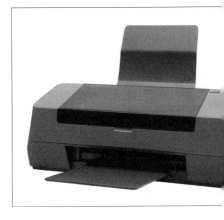

the computer and then printing the photo from the computer. Bingo bango – out come the photos! In the two years since I bought mine, I've probably printed somewhere between 24 and 27 photos. At this rate, I must be giving Boots a run for their money! That said, I never used to get my prints done at Boots in my pre-digital days. I was more of a Truprint man. The lure of a free film just made too much economic sense. Those Truprint days were happy ones and I do feel a little sad when I think about all the free films I've missed out on by converting to digital photography. But when all is said and done, the photo printer is a wonderful little piece of kit which offers convenience, quality and above all, photographic privacy. And in case I haven't mentioned it already, to use a photo printer you will need a computer.

RATING: 👍👍👍👍👍👍👍👍👍👍 10 thumbs up!

DIGITAL VIDEO RECORDER

Last night, I watched This Morning followed immediately by Hollyoaks (non-omnibus) followed immediately by Cash in the Attic. At first you might think this is impossible and presume that I am telling a lie. This Morning is a daytime show on ITV and Hollyoaks (non-omnibus) an early evening show on Channel 4, while Cash in the Attic is in the morning on BBC1

– they are non-sequential television programmes. Yet I am not telling a lie. Because I watched them on my Digital Video Recorder (DVR)! A DVR allows you to be Lord God of television. Not only can you record programmes but you can also pause live shows while you're watching! Just imagine the possibilities! If you're engrossed in the latest episode of QI and the urge to have a bathroom break becomes too much to postpone, you can simply freeze Stephen Fry mid-witticism. Or if you can't quite believe some of the dance moves that a teenage breakdancing boy has just done on Britain's Got Talent then you can rewind and take another look. The only downside is that sadly, even with one of these wonderful boxes, you can only watch programmes which have been on telly already, not ones which are yet to be screened. Still, I'm sure the boffins are working on that already!

RATING: 👍👍👍👍👍👍👍👍👍👍 10 thumbs up!

THE PAGER

For me, the pager (sometimes also known as the 'beeper') is possibly the greatest communications device created by mankind. Without the pager, I simply could not have functioned on a business or social level between the years of 1998 and 2001. I am deeply saddened that a generation has now grown up not knowing what a pager is. They probably think a mobile phone is the only device that has ever been used to receive text-based communications. They couldn't be more wrong. For me, a mobile phone 'text message' is simply not as personal as a 'page' and I'll tell you for why: when paging someone, you are required to dictate your message to a telephone operator, an actual physical person, who then turns it into a written message and sends it to the recipient. Now I believe that a message uttered by your lips is far more touching and genuine than a message typed by your thumbs. And as all the operators are skilled typists, a pager message is always correctly spelled and punctuated, unlike the lazy text speak which people seem to have adopted these days. Unfortunately, the world didn't share my more considered view and they adopted mobile phone technology instead. I still remember the day in January 2001 when my mobile phone company sent me a letter to inform me they would no longer be supporting pagers, so my unit would soon become obsolete. They sent me a £50 gift voucher as compensation which, to this day, sits in my bedside drawer, unused, as a protest against their shameful behaviour towards the pager (sometimes also known as the 'bleeper').

RATING: 👍👍👍👍👍👍👍👍👍👍 10 thumbs up!

UNIVERSAL REMOTE CONTROL

Up until last year, my living room was cluttered with three remote controls, for my TV (Television), DVD Player (Digital Versatile Disc Player) and Video Cassette Recorder (VCR). I used to sit on my sofa watching repeats of QI, becoming increasingly irked by the sight of so many devices and asking myself, 'Isn't there a better way?' Well there is – the 'Universal Remote Control'! It's a modest little thing – it looks like a single remote but behind this simplistic facade, it can actually control multiple consumer electronic devices. For example; TV, DVD Player, VCR, DVD Recorder, Freeview set-top box, Hifi system, DVD/VCR combo, portable TV, Home Cinema System. You name it, this little beauty can control it! Provided that it's a piece of consumer electronics which can be operated by an infra-red signal. And once you've got a Universal Remote, you can throw all those other remote controls away! Though please don't do that solely based on my advice. It might actually be best if you just put them in a kitchen drawer or some other similar place for safekeeping, just in case. Actually, come to think of it, should you wish to sell any of your electronic devices in the future, you will need the original remote controls so they can be included in the sale. So, on reflection, best not throw them away. Unless, of course, the purchaser also has a Universal Remote Control too, in which case you can throw them away!

RATING: 👍👍👍👍👍👍👍👍👍👍 10 thumbs up!

Gavin Shipman & Stacey West

Gavin Shipman, son of Michael and Pamela Shipman, and Stacey West, daughter of Trevor West (deceased) and Gwen West, got married abroad on 6th April 2007. The ceremony took place in St Nicholas's Church, Barry, South Wales. The happy couple got together after spending many hours talking with each other on the phone. It's no wonder they ended up engaged! So Gavin decided to 'Go West' while Stacey finally got her Ship-man! They're now off for a three-week honeymoon in Greece where they're bound to have a smashing time. They will return to live with Mr & Mrs Shipman in Billericay. The Billericay Herald would like to welcome Stacey Shipman to Essex. And while you can take the girl out of Barry, we're sure that you can't take Barry out of the girl. (Lucky fella, that Barry!)

Stacey West & Gavin Shipman

Stacey West, daughter of Trevor West (deceased) and Gwen West and niece of Bryn West, and Gavin Shipman, son of Mr & Mrs Shipman, were wed in St Nicholas's Church, on 6th April 2007. Stacey is a local girl who I'm sure we all know, while Gavin is a cockney boy from near London. Regular readers may also recognise Stacey from one or more of her five previous engagement announcements. The couple first courted each other on the phone and internet, which just goes to show that modern technology is not solely used for grooming children. For their honeymoon, they will be jetting off from this internationally famous beach resort of Barry to Greece.

IDEAS FOR GAVLAR'S STAG DO ATTENDEES

Me, Gavin, Gary n Simon, Budgie, Luggy,
Dirtbox, Fingers, ~~Jesus Mary, Rudi~~ Swede. / Mick? Jesus?
(Have t-shirt printers on standby in case Gav goes
soft and wants him along)

T-SHIRT IDEAS

Nicknames on all ~~polo shirts~~ T-shirts
That picture of Gav pulling moonie outside Ritzy's
Gav's face on back with 'Gavin Shipman RIP, 06.04.07'
Picture of Gav's face ~~clo~~ with speech bubble
'I'm in this club and up for bum gay sex.'
~~This is mine of this to sort out~~
Photo of Gav after Chinese Alan's stag do when we
wrote 'cock' on his head in marker pen

RULES

No phones ~~or letters~~
No birds (excludes ladies of the night)
No cameras
No pussying out at midnight
No soft drinks
Stag T-shirts compulsory at all times
What happens at the Stag Do stays at the Stag Do
Tell every girl who's interested in Fingers that he's gay

PLAN

1655 hours: Pick up minibus from Chris at the school. Wait till caretaker has left – he will say something to Pauline if he sees me driving it. ~~is but diri ill~~

17.00 hours: Phone Ritzy's to see if they're okay with stag parties.

18.00 hours: Lime Tree Avenue. Pam to provide berries and snacks (no need to ask, she will do it instinctively)

19.00 hours: Minibus to town. I'll drive it, then we can get taxis back. Make sure no one pukes – kids need it for field trip to Stansted Airport on Monday.

19.30 hours: Yates's. Get in early. Get a big ~~table~~. Get leathered.

22.30 hours: ~~Back up plan~~ Back up plan. If I forgot to check with Ritzy's about stag parties, just go there early to beat the queue.

23.30 hours: Back up plan. Go to Ritzy's now if we forgot to go early.

00.00 hours: Back up plan. If Ritzy's don't let in stag parties, go to Roxy's. They can't afford to be picky these, we'll deffo get in.

00.30 hours: Back up plan. If Roxy's are picky about stag parties, retire to the minibus. Dish out the spare jumpers to everyone to cover stag T-shirts. Send the boys back to Roxy's in parties of two. ~~Really i will what we this out~~

01.00 hours: All of us reconvene in the R'n'B room for some b-boy stylings.

02.00 hours: Head over to T&A's and check out the kebabs.

03.00 hours: Head over to Private Dancers and check out some more kebabs!! ~~nipples~~

04.00 hours: Back to Lime Tree Avenue in taxis. Catering courtesy of Pamela – leftovers in the fridge.

09.00 hours: (just Smithy) Get cab back to minibus. Drive minibus to school. Stay to watch Lucy's Youth Orchestra playing at fete.

<u>Best man speech</u>

First of all I'd like to raise a toast (hold up piece of toast) to the happy couple.

I'll never forget when me and Gav was at the football and we was eating these hot dogs and I dropped mine on the floor. Gutted. And Gav said to me 'Smithy. Have mine'. And I was touched. What a beautiful gesture from a true mate – it was like that song 'Two Little Boys'. Then after I finished eating Gav's hot dog, he turned to me and said 'Smithy. Mate. I dropped that one on the floor too'. Bastard! I always said I'd get him back for that. So, Gavlar, (hold up poloraid photo) ~~get this pens~~ recognise this Goat's Cheese Tartlet sitting on the hotel carpet? ~~You should do this for~~ ~~me if you haven't yet~~. You should do, son, you just ate it! (pause for laugh) ~~No~~

But ~~really~~ seriously, Gav and me have been mates since we were 4, and over the years I've picked up more dirt on this boy than you can (hold up stick and wave it) shake a ~~stick at this I say~~. stick at. Some of it's really filthy. Honestly, if Stacey heard it, she might rethink...

(Moo!)

Anyway, as this is a family event I ain't gonna use blue language. So to keep it clean, I'll just leave it at this. In his time, Gav's had to take a few of these (hold up Viagras), ~~pills in the~~ e had his fair share of these (put on moose mask), I'm talking about Kelly, she was a moose! And he's and even ended up with a case of these (hold up plastic crabs). I've been ~~scratching to do this~~ itching to do that one! Itching! (pause for laugh)

But seriously, for those of you who don't know Gav, he's a top bloke. Kind, generous and funny. Stacey's lucky she found him - though with five engagements under his belt, it's less about luck and more trial and error, ~~I ttter~~ eh Stace? Five fiances in a row! (put on arrow through head hat) A-row? Arrow? Yeah? (hopefully pause for laugh. Though not 100% ~~sseme~~

But seriously, Stacey's a lovely girl and her and Gav are made for each other. I haven't known her long, but anyone can see how much they're in love. ~~this is the most important thing to remember. Bes.~~   The most important thing is that Stacey's made our Gavin as happy as (hold up picture of Larry Hagman) JR. I'm joking! Larry Hagman - happy ~~as Herry~~ as Larry!

~~Obviously~~ though, there's a couple of best man duties I need to get out of the way before I finish. Firstly, all the brides-maids were awesome. Also I must say that we've all had a quality day, so I just want to thank the person who's laid all this on for us today – Gwen (wink at Pam). Believe me Gwen, you're gonna wish you hadn't laid on a free bar when you ~~catch~~ see the Smithsters in action later on...

But seriously, now that he's a married man, I know Gav won't be spending as much time with me and the boys. But he'll always be ~~my mate and I'll always~~ ~~forever be best friends the end!~~ my mate and I'll always be interested in what's going on in his life – so I hope he keeps me abreast (Hold up plastic boobs) of what's going on in his life! This isn't the only pair you'll be staring at tonight, Gavlar!

To the bride and groom!

NORTHERN UNION
(THE NORTHERN UNION TELEGRAPH COMPANY)
CABLEGRAM

2007 APR 6

ANGLO-CELTIC TELEGRAPH CO. LD.   **BRITISH NATIONAL TELEGRAPHS.**

M657 BARRY ISLAND 408 10 1310 –

STACEY AND GAVIN SHIPMAN

ST. NICHOLAS'S CHURCH –

HELLO STOP BRYN HERE STOP I AM SENDING YOU A
WEDDING TELEGRAM STOP CAN YOU BELIEVE IT? THEY
STILL DO THEM STOP I DID NOT THINK THEY WOULD
STOP THEY DO COST A FAIR PENNY BUT IT IS WORTH
IT STOP OBVIOUSLY I AM THERE BY YOUR SIDE BUT
I JUST THOUGHT I WOULD SEND YOU A TELEGRAM
AS A JOKE STOP THE MAN I AM TALKING TO SAYS
HAVE A LOVELY WEDDING =

BRYN

NORTHERN UNION
(THE NORTHERN UNION TELEGRAPH COMPANY)
CABLEGRAM

ANGLO-CELTIC TELEGRAPH CO. LD.   BRITISH NATIONAL TELEGRAPHS.

M657 BARRY ISLAND 408 10 1330 -

STACEY AND GAVIN SHIPMAN

ST. NICHOLAS'S CHURCH -

HELLO STOP DAVID BECKHAM HERE STOP BRYN TOLD
ME IT WAS YOUR WEDDING DAY STOP SO I THOUGHT
I WOULD SEND YOU A TELEGRAM TO SAY HAVE A GOOD
ONE STOP ME AND VICTORIA SEND OUR BEST STOP
ONLY JOKING STOP IT IS ME STOP BRYN STOP
I THOUGHT I WOULD SEND THIS ONE AS A JOKE
TOO STOP ALTHOUGH IF DAVID BECKHAM KNEW YOU
WERE GETTING MARRIED I AM SURE HE WOULD SEND
HIS BEST STOP =
BRYN

Community Notes

Father Chris' THOUGHTS FOR THE DAY

In the beginning there was the word, and the word was God. Not 'Harry Potter' or 'Britney Spears'. Not 'Playstation 360' or 'Facebooks'. God. And although it started with one word, we have to use many 'words' to describe all the things he's done for us. These are my 'Thoughts for the Day'.

I was watching the Pop-Factor last Saturday. At one point two attractive young ladies came on and started to remove their clothes. Simon Cowell did not know where to look, I can tell you. The girl judge was very quick to press her button. 'I'm out' she said. And Mr. Cowell soon pressing his too. Piers Morgan just kept watching. Transfixed by the undressing ladies. Luckily the dancing ladies stopped just before it got too naughty!! But if you think about it, there was also another man who was 'tempted' like Piers Morgan. Many years ago, in the wilderness, Jesus was approached by the Devil and asked to perform all manner of acts. Unlike Piers Morgan, Jesus pressed his big red button and voted the Devil off the stage. 'No Satan! You will not be going through to the semi-final!' he exclaimed! So in many ways that girl who sits in the middle is like the mother Mary, trying to protect her son. And Simon Cowell is like Jesus. When he speaks his mind he is persecuted by the audience, just like our saviour. But yet he still carries on, travelling the world and delivering his message. Telling us that there is hope for all of us to achieve our potential. In his own words : 'You could be Nancy.' With God's help, we can all be Nancies.

Yesterday I watched my grandson steal a car, run over three pedestrians and shoot a prostitute in the head – ten times! Yet somehow he's not in prison. Why? Because he was playing a computer game. Car Theft Auto. He ended up with the computer police on his trail. So he just drove and drove. Eventually he got away from them and the search for my dangerous grandson was called off. Unfortunately he took his girlfriend to a strip bar and killed all the strippers with a hand grenade, as she looked on. Guess what – yet again the computer police were on his trail! After mowing down a hotdog salesman and stealing his money, he managed to evade capture a second time. He was no longer wanted by the police and could walk around without fear of them shooting at him. And that's a bit like God. No matter what you do, God will always forgive you if you simply 'run away from the police'. Or as Christians call it – 'repent'. If you've told a lie, repent and God will forgive you. If you've stolen, repent and God will forgive you. If you've killed a stripper with a rocket launcher, repent and God will forgive you. Simply 'run away from the police' in your life and God will welcome you onto life's final 'level' – the kingdom of heaven.

You know what I'm looking forward to this year? The Glastonbury festival. You may well look at me and think 'How does an old fuddy-duddy like Father Chris know about the Glastonbury festival?' Well I have read a thing or two about it in the supplements. Let me explain how it works. It's a pop concert with lots of 'wicked' bands playing. Coolplay, Britney Spears, Duran Duran, The Radioheads – I bet they're all doing a turn this year. Apparently there are so many exciting things to do and see that you simply can't do them all. Yes, you get a bit muddy. Yes, the toilets are apparently horrible. But at the end of the day everyone gets together at the Glastonbury stage and watches one band. 'The headliner'. Do you realize how similar that is to the Christian faith? Us Christians come in all different flavours – Protestant, Catholic, Methodist etc. So much choice! But at the end of the day we all meet up to watch the same show. Except our 'Headliner' is God, the chemical toilets are the hard times, Michael Eavis is Jesus and the trendy bands are the 12 disciples. You can even 'get high'; not by smoking hashish but by smoking a big fat joint of God's love. For we are all part of God's big festival. You are all part of God-stonbury!

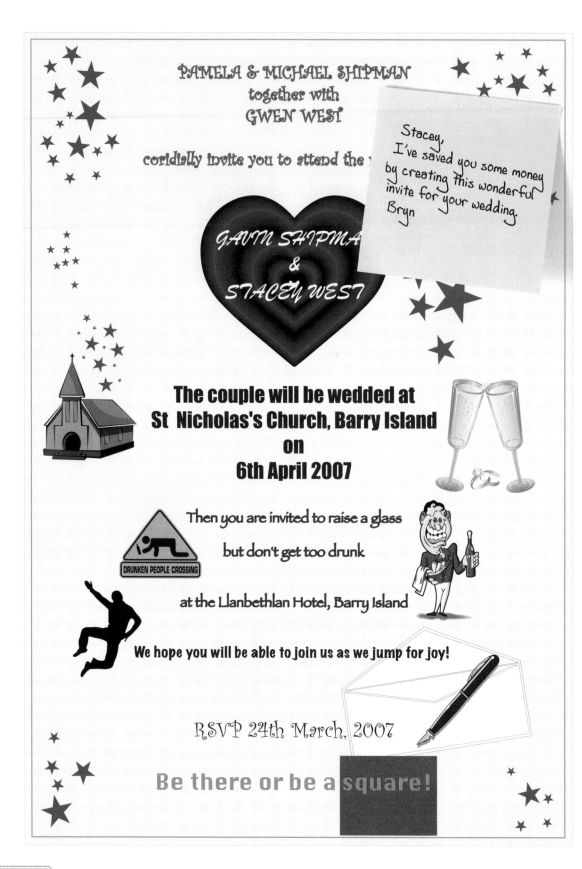

PAMELA & MICHAEL SHIPMAN
together with
GWEN WEST

coridially invite you to attend the

Stacey,
I've saved you some money by creating this wonderful invite for your wedding.
Bryn

GAVIN SHIPMAN
&
STACEY WEST

**The couple will be wedded at
St Nicholas's Church, Barry Island
on
6th April 2007**

Then you are invited to raise a glass

but don't get too drunk

DRUNKEN PEOPLE CROSSING

at the Llanbethlan Hotel, Barry Island

We hope you will be able to join us as we jump for joy!

RSVP 24th March, 2007

Be there or be a square!

Pamela & Michael Shipman

together with

Gwen West

cordially invite you to attend the marriage of

Gavin Shipman

&

Stacey West

The couple will be wedded at

St Nicholas's Church, Barry Island

on

6th April 2007

Then you are invited to raise a glass

at the Llanbethlan Hotel, Barry Island

We hope you will be able to join us.

RSVP 24th March, 2007

St Nicholas's Church, Barry

Order of Service
for the marriage of

Gavin Shipman

&

Stacey West

6th April 2007 at 1.00pm

Service conducted by Father Chris

ARRIVAL

Bridal March

HYMN: JERUSALEM

Words by William Blake, Music by C. Hubert H. Parry

Nice one, Gavlar – stick it to the taffs, son! England 1, Wales 0

And did those feet in ancient time

Walk upon England's mountain green?

And was the holy Lamb of God

Must mean Mick's lamb. Now that is the lamb of God. What a marinade.

On England's pleasant pastures seen?

And did the countenance divine

Shine forth upon our clouded hills?

And was Jerusalem builded here

Schoolboy error, Blakey boy, the word is 'built'

Among those dark satanic mills?

Bring me my bow of burning gold!

Bring me my arrows of desire!

Bring me my spear! O clouds, unfold!

Anything else you want me to

Bring me my chariot of fire!

bring you while I'm at it?

I will not cease from mental fight,

Mental fights? This is Barry. They're everywhere

Nor shall my sword sleep in my hand,

I've had my sword in my hand three times in the last 24 hours. Definitely wasn't sleeping.

Till we have built Jerusalem

that's better, Blakey boy

In England's green and pleasant land.

ENG-ER-LAND!

THE MARRIAGE CEREMONY

He does. She does. Get a wriggle on, yeah?

FC 1, WEST HAM 6

READING

Read by Vanessa Jenkins, Maid of Honour

Who's Vanessa?

HYMN – BREAD OF HEAVEN

Words by William Williams *Williams William*
William Williams

Music by John Hughes

We're gonna be here till Songs of Praise is on at this rate. Fuck's sake.

Guide me, O Thou great Jehovah,	When I tread the verge of Jordan,
Pilgrim through this barren land	Bid my anxious fears subside;
I am weak, but Thou art mighty;	Death of death and hell's destruction,
Hold me with Thy powerful hand.	Land me safe on Canaan's side.

dirty bastard!

Bread of heaven, bread of heaven,	Songs of praises, songs of praises,
Feed me till I want no more	I will ever give to Thee
Feed me till I want no more.	I will ever give to Thee.

Talking of which, can we hurry up and get to the reception. I'm Hank Marvin!

Verse four? Piss take.

Open now the crystal fountain,	Musing on my habitation,
Whence the healing stream doth flow;	Musing on my heav'nly home,
Let the fire and cloudy pillar	Fills my soul with holy longings:
Lead me all my journey through.	Come, my Jesus, quickly come;
Strong deliverer, strong deliverer,	Vanity is all I see;
Be Thou still my strength and shield	Lord, I long to be with Thee!
Be Thou still my strength and shield.	Lord, I long to be with Thee!

And hence forth Gavlar will be show-eth-ing Stace his cloudy pillar ...

And hence forth, Gav will be filling Stacey's soul with his holy longing ...

dirty bastard!

Hang on? We never done this verse at school. How much longer?

PRAYERS

Dear Lord. Please don't let Nessa be sitting next to me at the reception. Amen

SPECIAL PERFORMANCE BY VANESSA JENKINS

'Still the one' by Shania Twain

Amazing, for all the wrong reasons...

SIGNING OF THE REGISTER

Please remain seated while the register is signed.

Music will be provided by Chill Out Sessions 2004 by

The Ministry of Sound *Tunee!*

WEDDING MARCH

THANKS

Thanks to...

Read? she can barely speak proper English

Nessa for being Maid of Honour and her reading

Smithy for being Best Man

Bryn for walking Stacey down the aisle

All our friends and family for being with
us on this special day

Stace – when you throw the bouquet – aim for me. Because I will elbow people out of the way to get it if I have to. Louise.

There were only three types of beer at the bar I thought you would at least have a selection of all the beers from around the world. Outrage! Have a good one! Garry 'n' Simon

HAVE A GOOD HONEY MOON MATE – DON'T DO ANYTHING (WOULDN'T DO. SO THAT DOESN'T REALLY RULE OUT ANYTHING.(!!) WISHING YOU GUYS ALL THE BEST! CRAIG (RANGERS)

I rememb-
threw
hesita
eve
fif

Sorry I missed you at the hen night. I was running like a gooduni I thought it was best to leave because. I think it's bad luck to be sick on the bride. Erin

Trevor would be proud of you both. Gwen.

y honeymoon — my husband
 the bed and without
e were at it like rabbits —
ich way! But that was the
imes change. So God knows what
kids get up to now-a-days.
how, have a great time, Doris.

Very well done. I have taken a lot of photos. The first few were in "fine" quality, but I was running out of memory on my camera so I had to reduce the quality to "normal". Don't worry — they look okay!
Bryn

yet again, I hope you two are very happy together. I continue to be wishing you all the best. Griff

LOVED THE BEST MAN'S SPEECH- BIG BABY! BUT SERIOUSLY. I'M REALLY ENJOYING MYSELF. WELL DONE GUYS. LUGGY

Yo Gav —
Now you're married does this mean you're gonna finally have sex.
Budgie

Again, I hope you have a very happy together. I wish you all the best yet again. Griff

To the love birds! By the time you read this I'll have done my best man speech. Can't wait for you to see it. You will laugh your tits off! Will pass this book round after the wedding breakfast.

(Finally, breakfast served at the proper time! 2pm!!)

Gavin you look after my little sis else there'll therell be trouble! I hope you have a long and happy life together!

Jason

MY DAD, GOD, SAYS NICE BIT OF SKIRT GOOD EFFORT, MY SON!, HEH-HEH! JESUS

Gavin
my lit
troubl
long

Stacey looked amazing in that dress — but she'd look even better if it had a paintball mark on the back of it! What do you say. Bride's side versus Grooms. — Fingers.

MAY THE ROADS RISE UP TO MEET YOU.
MAY THE SUN BE ALWAYS AT YOUR BACK. TIDY.
NESS

I hope you two are very happy together I wish you all the best.
Griff

you look after
sis else there'll be
I hope you have a
and happy life together

Jason

Stace looked amazing in that
dress - but she'd look even
better if it had paintball marks
on it! What do you say? Bride's
side verses Groom's? Swede

Hey Gav
How come Griff
gets to sign it
three times? Is he
your new bum chum?
Dirtbox

After playing Smithy's "Cruise,
Marry, Shag" game I feel you both now
know the answer to all three: each other.

Mick

As a married man
I'd just like to say -
you two should both
get out of it! Get out
of it! As quickly as
you can! Only joking
It's Awesome. Chinese Alan.

Oh Mick! Gav won't want you talking
about him shagging Stace. You're his
Dad! It was a very beautiful day.
Thank you for letting us pay for just
about everything at your wedding.
Our money was well spent! Pam

Hey Mum,

Oh my god!! Greece is lush!! I am having a wonderful time. Our hotel is amazing and so's Gav. It has everything. Swimming pool, a TV ... it's the lap of luxury. Food is amazing - although we went out to get a kebab and couldn't find one anywhere. I said to Gav 'Here we are in Greece and not a kebab van in sight'. Shocked, I was. Yesterday the waiters found out it was our honeymoon and they sang to us and we got to smash some plates - then everyone joined in. Unfortunately there was a bit of an incident: some fella was rushed off to hospital. Something to do with a piece of cutlery and his arm. Anyway it was all very exciting.

The hotel has a spa!! So I went down and had a hot stone massage followed by a go in the 'Flotation Tank'. You're supposed to be in there for an hour to let your mind and spirit clear totally. Got out after five minutes. Boring as hell, it was. My head kept bumping into the wall.

Tell you what though, I do miss home. I haven't had a proper cup of tea in ages. The milk tastes funny here. Send my love to Bryn and Nessa. I'm off to have a drink in the swimming pool! I know!! They have a bar in the swimming pool!! Lush!

From,
'Mrs Shipman' (I'm never going to get used to that!)

Gwen West

62 Holbot Road

Barry Island

South Glamorgan

Wales

Wish you were here!

Welcome to Greece

CARTE POSTALE

AIR MAIL

Nessa,
You were right about the toilets. I took one step
inside a public one and was almost sick. So I'm
not drinking much and holding it in all day and
then going in the hotel.

The food's lovely, but we really struggled yesterday. It was 5 o'clock and me and Gav fancied
some nosh. But get this, all the restaurants were
closed. Weird, it was. Most of them don't open till
8! So we went to Maccie D's instead and had a
deli sandwich.

The restaurants only take cash too. Don't ask why.
It's madness. First day we got here, we only had
20 euro on us, so me and Gav just shared one
starter, one main and one beer. Didn't leave a
tip. Now we have to avoid that restaurant. Shame.
Lovely food.

I'm going to stop writing this now as I need a pee
... and it's a half an hour walk back to the hotel.

I love you Ness,
Stace

P.S. Say hi to Noel and the rest of the ???

Nessa Jenkins

43 Holbot Road

Barry Island

South Glamorgan

Wales

Mum and Dad,

me and Stace are having a wonderful
time. Hotel's amazing. Swimming Pool,
Sky Sports 1, 2, 3 and News. Spa
for Stace. Sky Movies. This place
has got everything. These Greeks have
really got it down — you get up at
10am then you go to bed at 2pm, then
you get up at 5pm. It's like being
unemployed.
Everyone's being really nice. The hotel
staff knew we're on honeymoon and so
they folded up the towels to look like
swans. Don't want to disturb them so
we're using our own.
Must admit, I am getting a bit fed
up of fish and music that gets
faster and faster. Looking forward
to getting home 'cos the milk tastes a
bit funny here.
Anyway, I'll bring you back a
smashed plate or something.
Love, Gav

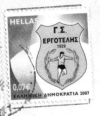

17 Lime Tree Avenue

Billericay, Basildon

Essex SS14 2EZ

England

Beautiful Greece

Girls of Greece

Smithster!

You would not believe it. Here I've been
telling Stace how much you'd love it.
Apart from the local beers — they're all a
bit shit really — but I'm gonna bring back
a bottle of that beer we read about in
Nuts magazine. I promise I won't drink
any before I see you.
It's really weird, lots of people gob
everywhere. Stace won't let me join in.
She says it's okay to act like the locals
'When in Rome' but we're in Greece so
we've got to act like British tourists.
Did I mention, we got Sky Sports 1, 2, 3,
News AND Sky movies. Watched the
Spurs game on Sunday. In Greece! Mental.
Plus I've been doing that thing you said.
Every time I see a menu I've been shaking
my head and saying 'It's all Greek to me'.
I've done it 8 times. I don't think it will
ever stop being funny.
You probably won't get this till after I get
back. Partly because the postmen here are
probably asleep all day, and partly
because I'm writing this at the airport.
Gavlar.

CARTE POSTALE

VIA AIR MAIL

HELLAS
ΕΛΛΗΝΙΚΗ ΔΗΜΟΚΡΑΤΙΑ
2007

Smithster
35 Lime Tree Avenue
Billericay, Basildon
Essex SS14 2EZ

ENGLAND

NESSA'S

Birthing Tips

Alrigh', so giving birth is no easy ride (that's the thing that got you into this mess in the first place), but there are ways you can make the whole experience a bit more pleasant. Now, having been through it myself, which I has, there are a few hints and tips which I want to pass on to those less fortunate than me, i.e. pregnant women. At the end of the day, if by doing this I can make just one person's birth experience better then, quite frankly, it's not been worth my bother.

DON'T BE PANICKING

When the contractions start, don't be panicking. There's several hours to go yet and, I won't lie to you, it's gonna get very boring before it gets very painful. So watch a video. Unfortunately, I was staying at Gwen's when I went into labour so there wasn't a lot of choice. I ended up watching the box set of Soldier, Soldier series seven (after Robson and Jerome). I tell you what, three episodes of that and the prospect of labour in't so scary.

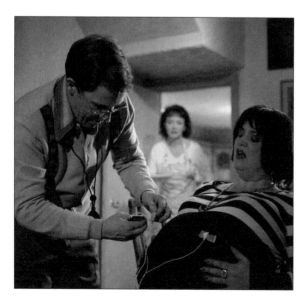

KEEP YOUR ENERGY UP

You're going to need a lot of energy so make sure you feed yourself up on energetic foods. No word of a lie, Kevin Keegan himself told me that pound for pound, Jaffa Cakes are the best energy food on earth. And drink a bit of Lucozade Sport. But save some for afterwards – after 19 hours of sheer hell, you're gonna be thirsty. You could also have a couple of omelettes. For what it's worth, flavour-wise, my preference was plain. Your baby's got a big enough shock coming without having to tackle a fussy omelette for its last meal in captivity.

PICK A TIDY PARTNER

If the babyfather ain't around then you're gonna have to pick someone else as a birthing partner. But think carefully about who you want in there with you. I had two key criteria, which stood me in good stead: a) Will they be supportive? b) Am I bothered about them seeing me downstairs? Stace ticked both boxes.

TIDY ATMOSPHERE

It helps to have a relaxing atmosphere in the room, so have a think about what music you want to listen to. I won't lie to you, the drifty vocals of Jack Johnson were a big help to me. I also listened to James Blunt, Jamiroquai and Ja Rule, but that's only 'cos Bryn couldn't work the shuffle function on his iPod. Aromatherapy can be helpful too. Nutmeg, geranium and lavender were all recommended to me, but personally I opted for Airwick's Rose Garden. That particular scent made me feel extremely relaxed, particularly when I smelled the aerosol up close.

GET PAIN RELIEF

When it comes to pain relief, when all's said and done, I would say it's best not to rely on agricultural methods. While Dave bringing along a machine normally used on cattle was very thoughtful and economical, it probably wasn't the time to be experimenting with electrical currents. My advice would be that if the midwives offer you any kind of pain relief then take it. And stash half of it for another time. Especially the diamorphine. Some of my best nights out in Barry have been thanks to diamorphine.

And that's it. Simple as. At the end of the day, there's six billion people on the planet so you ain't the first one to bang out a nipper. So just get on with it.

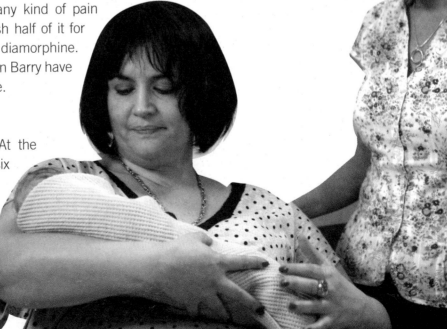

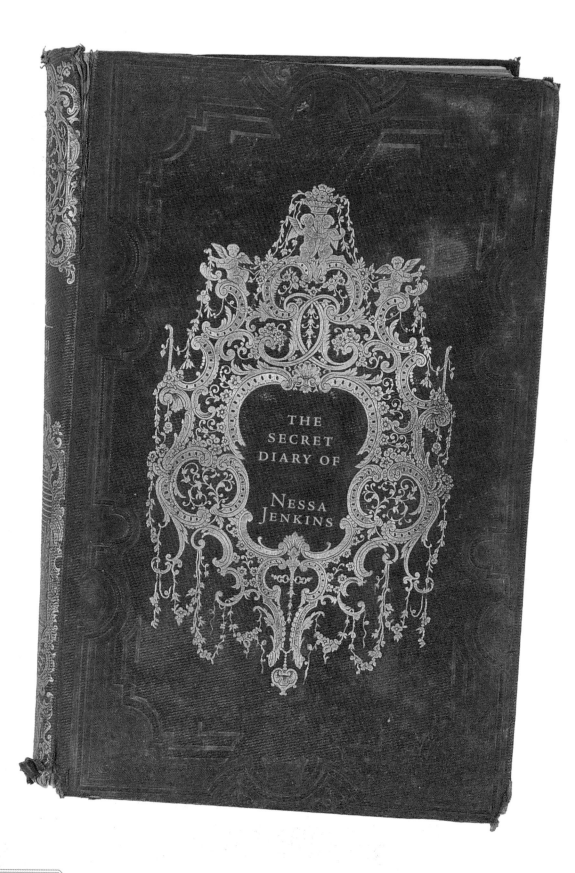

THE
SECRET
DIARY OF

NESSA
JENKINS

AUGUST 23RD 1980

O DIARY.

TODAY SHOULD'VE BEEN ONE OF THE HAPPIEST DAYS OF MY LIFE, BUT I'M NOT GONNA LIE TO YOU - IT WAS A JOKE. I WOKE UP, IN VEGAS, IN BED WITH TWO OF GLADYS KNIGHT'S PIPS. NICE FELLAS - DON'T GET ME WRONG - BUT IT SHOULD'VE BEEN EMRYS. GOD KNOWS WHERE HE'S DISAPPEARED TO - LAST TIME I SAW HIM HE WAS DRINKING TEQUILA FROM THE HOLLOW OF A CROUPIER'S PALM. IT WAS A HEAVY NIGHT, OF COURSE IT WAS - WE'D JUST GOT MARRIED, WHAT MORE D'YOU EXPECT. AND SEEING GLADYS WAS A BONUS - SHE WAS DOING A SHORT SET THERE AS A FAVOUR TO THE CASINO BOSS, ROBERT DENARIO. ME AND GLAD GO BACK A LONG WAY - I WAS HER DRIVER FOR A SHORT WHILE BACK IN '79. HAPPY DAYS. SO IT MADE SENSE THAT WE SHOULD SHARE A FEW MARTINIS, TALK ABOUT OLD TIMES. I GAVE HER A BIT OF IMAGE THERAPY - SHE WAS HAVIN' A FEW PROBLEMS WITH HER WEIGHT AT THE TIME AND I WAS ONLY TOO GLAD TO HELP HER OUT. BUT AFTER THAT IT ALL GOT MESSY. EM WENT OFF THE RAILS AND UNDER THE RADAR, AND BEFORE I KNEW IT ME AND A PIP (I FORGET WHICH ONE - TALL AND GINGER) WERE CONSOLING EACH OTHER BACK AT THE MOTEL. THE OTHER PIP TURNED UP LATER, HE'D LOST HIS KEY. EMRYS, IF YOU'RE READING THIS, WHICH IS HIGHLY UNLIKELY GIVEN THAT IT'S MY DIARY, GET IN TOUCH. YOU STILL OWE ME TWENTY QUID.

TAKEN FROM NESSA'S
DIARY THE DAY OF
HER FIRST WEDDING

MARCH 13TH 1982

O DIARY.

I'M VERY WORRIED ABOUT CAROLE. WE WENT TO ST DAVID'S
HALL TONIGHT TO SEE GARY. NUMAN. HE'D GIVEN US A COUPLE
OF VIP STAGE PASSES WHICH ISN'T SURPRISING GIVEN THAT
I'M GODMOTHER TO HIS COUSIN'S CHILD. ANYWAY, SHE WAS OUT
OF SORTS ALL NIGHT - SHE'S A BIG GIRL, BIGGER THAN ME, SO
SHE DOES PUFF A LOT WHICH MAKES IT SOUND LIKE SHE'S
BORED WHEN SHE'S NOT. BUT WHEN WE WENT TO GARY'S
DRESSING ROOM SHE WAS RESTLESS. KEPT LOOKING AT HER
WATCH. I FOUND IT QUITE RUDE IF TRUTH BE TOLD, AND SO
DID GAZ. HE KNEW THE SCORE, I COULD TELL. HE FIXED ME WITH
ONE OF HIS STARES - HE CAN BE QUITE DISTURBING AT TIMES,
I WON'T LIE TO YOU - AND ASKED ME "ARE FRIENDS ELECTRIC?"
IN A KIND OF MEANINGFUL WAY. ANYWAY, CAROLE MADE IT
VERY CLEAR THAT SHE WAS READY TO GO. GARY WANTED HIS
DRIVER TO TAKE US HOME BUT CAROLE HAD DIFFERENT IDEAS.
IT SOON BECAME CLEAR AS TO WHY. WAITIN' OUTSIDE IN HIS
AUSTIN ALLEGRO WAS JOCKIE. HER FELLA. SCOTTISH. QUITE
STUNTED. AND IN THE BACK SEAT WAS A SHIFTY LOOKIN'
BLOKE FROM MOROCCO. TINY EYES. I DIDN'T LIKE THE LOOK OF
HIM TO BE HONEST. AND HE NEVER SPOKE A WORD WHICH DIDN'T
HELP. IN FACT NO-ONE SAID ANYTHING ON THE WAY BACK.
THEY JUST DROPPED ME OFF AT THE DOLPHIN AND WENT
ON THEIR MERRY WAY. I WATCHED THEM GO. HEADING NORTH
THEY WERE. I GOT A FEELING SHE WON'T BE COMIN' BACK.

JUNE 17TH 2003

O DIARY.

I'VE DONE IT. I'VE LEFT JOHN. I COULDN'T TAKE IT NO
MORE AND BARRY WAS CALLIN'. ISLAND, NOT WHITE. THO'
WEIRDLY HE'S BEEN IN TOUCH A BIT OF LATE AN' ALL.
FUNNY HOW THEY CAN NEVER QUITE LET GO ..., I HOPE
JOHN CAN. WE'RE DESTROYIN' EACH OTHER: THE WINING
AND THE DININ' AND MORE DININ' - I HAD TO GET OUT. I
HITCHED A LIFT TO VICTORIA AND GOT MYSELF ON THE
509 TO CARDIFF. I KNOW I COULD'VE TAKEN THE JAG BUT
WHY KICK A MAN WHEN HE'S DOWN. HE LOVES THAT CAR.

JUNE 18TH, 2003

O DIARY.

JOHN'S TAKEN IT BAD APPARENTLY. HE'S GONE MENTAL
AND HE NEEDS HELP. I'VE ASKED DAVE B TO KEEP AN
EYE ON HIM FOR ME, MAKE SURE HE DON'T DO NOTHIN'
STUPID LIKE PUNCH A MEMBER OF THE VOTING PUBLIC.

THE NIGHT NESSA
LEFT JOHN PRESCOTT.

FEB 23RD 1994

O DIARY.

SHAZNAY IS DOIN MY HEAD IN. SHE'S NOW CLAIMIN' SHE
WROTE THE LYRICS TO "NEVER EVER". THE GIRL'S
DELUDED. SHE CAME UP WITH THE TITLE IF TRUTH
BE TOLD AND THAT WAS HARDLY ROCKET SCIENCE.
I TOLD HER TO BACK OFF THIS MORNING. EITHER SHE
WANTS MY ARTISTIC INPUT OR SHE DON'T COS I KNOW
WHERE IT'S AT. I'VE SPOKEN TO MEL AND NIC ABOUT
IT AND THEY TOTALLY SYMPATHIZE. NAT'S STILL
ON THE FENCE WHICH IS FAIR ENOUGH GIVEN WHAT'S
GONE ON IN THE PAST. BUT I TELL YOU, IF THIS SHIT
CARRIES ON I'M GETTING' OUT. I GOT MORE SELF
RESPECT THAN TO HANG AROUND IN A GIRL-BAND THE
REST OF MY LIFE. I'LL GO SOLO IF I HAVE TO. SIMPLE AS.

ON LEAVING ALL SAINTS.

AFT OF SONG

S THAT I ~~SHINE~~ WANT TO KNOW
EVE' HURT ME SO CHANGE
ELIEVE THAT I WAS WRONG
LONG THIS BEEN GOING ON
NEVER PAY ENOUGH ATTENTION
HEAD?
NOT GIVE ENOUGH AFFECTION IN BE

NGE

APRIL 2ND 2007

O DIARY.

WELL THAT'S IT THEN. I'M DEFO WITH CHILD.
DOCTOR SAID LIKE. AND 'S' IS DEFO THE DAD. I'M
GUTTED. I CAN'T TELL STACE. NOT WITH
THE WEDDIN' AN' WHAT HAVE YOU. I'M THINKING
ABOUT THE 'ALTERNATIVE ROUTE' AND I DON'T
THINK I CAN FACE IT. SO I WENT TO BLOCKBUSTERS
AND GOT VERA DRAKE OUT ON DVD. I'LL TAKE IT
ROUND BRYN'S TOMORROW. HE LOVES THAT IMELDA
STAUNTON SO HE WON'T THINK ANYTHING OF
IT. OH CHRIST. WHAT THE HELL AM I GONNA DO?

APRIL 3RD 2007

O DIARY

I'M KEEPIN' THE BABY. I'VE DECIDED. IT WAS THE FILM
THAT DONE IT IN THE END. WE HAD TO WATCH IT
TWICE COS BRYN DIDN'T GET THE PLOT.

ON FINDING OUT
SHE'S PREGNANT.

JANUARY 27TH 2001

O DIARY.

THOUGHT I SAW PAULO TODAY, DOWN

BARRY MAGS. I DIDN'T. IT WASN'T HIM.

THE DAY SHE THOUGHT
SHE SAW PAULO, HER ONLY
TRUE LOVE, DOWN BARRY
MAGISTRATES COURT.

1ST FEB 2007

O DIARY,

WENT LONDON TODAY WITH STACE. MET HER
COCKNEY FELLA. NICE KID, I'M NOT GONNA LIE TO
YOU. JUST WISH I COULD SAY THE SAME ABOUT
HIS MATE. WE DID IT - OF COURSE WE DID. IN
THE ENSUITE. AND I GOT TO BE HONEST IT
WAS A PLEASANT SURPRIZE. I DIDN'T THINK
HE HAD IT IN HIM. MIND YOU, I STILL THINK HE
HAD IT IN HIM WHEN I LEFT THE NEXT DAY.
NOT A LOT ELSE GOING FOR HIM MIND. CAN'T
EVEN REMEMBER HIS NAME. AND I WON'T BE
SEEING HIM AGAIN THAT'S FOR SURE. BUS
BACK. CURRY WITH DAVE DOWN HIS. TIDY.

THE DAY AFTER SHE
MET SMITHY

And finally...

Bryn's favourite jokes

I count myself very lucky in life as every now and again, I get sent wonderful emails filled with jokes or perhaps with hilarious pictures attached. Some of these jokes are simply brilliant. As funny as anything you see on telly from Ant and Dec or Brian Conley. Well, I often find myself wanting to fill an awkward silence at a social occasion with a hilarious one-liner, and as such I thought it would be a good idea to write down all of the best ones rather than simply delete them and risk losing them forever. This collection has won me dozens of friends and got several parties started, I can tell you!

A fella went in to the bakers and Jordan walks out. The man says 'No! I Just asked for a small orange tart!'

I went to the pet shop the other day. But they wouldn't let me have the deal in the window. Even though it quite clearly said: 'Dog-Pound'.

What do you call an English woman with long sharp objects on her legs?
Brit Knee-Spears.

How many procrastinators does it take to change a light bulb?
Look, can I tell you later?

How do you revive a funeral? Just wait till it's a-wake.

What's got a long mane and 'neighs' a lot? Russell Brand.

A man went to the doctors. The doctor put his hand on the man's testicles and asked him if he wouldn't mind coughing. 'Coughing?', the man replied, 'with your hand round them I'll do anything you bloody want!'

'Doctor Doctor I'm seeing double'. 'There doesn't seem to be anything wrong with you. Did you want a second opinion?' 'No, I just got one thanks.'

Two men are rowing the English Channel, one says to the other, 'What currency do they use in France?' 'Euro,' the other replies. The man shrugs. 'Oh alright, give us the oars then.'

What's tall, grey and stands in the middle of Trafalgar square?
An elephant on holiday.

What do you call a vampire ape?
An orang-u-fang.

What's the fastest fish in the ocean?
Sea Bass-tian Coe.

Which illness can fly?
Flu.
What do you call festive ducks?
Christmas Quackers.

Tony has bigger lungs than Miranda. And Carla has larger lungs than Tony. Who can expel the largest amount of air through their mouth?
None of them. They're all the same sighs.

What do you call a female millionaire who always wants to pass wind?
Ivana Trump.

A man asked his friend 'Do you want me to give you a pound?',
The friend said 'Yes'.
The man hit his friend in the arm.
'There you go. Do you want another one?'

What do farmers put in their fields to look after birds?
Care-crows.

How many optimists does it take to change a light bulb?
None. The light bulb won't need changing.

What do you call a Boeing 747 that's going bald?
A 'receding 'airline'.

What do you call someone who's prejudiced against floors?
Florist.

Where do nuns go after dinner?
Nun-eaton.

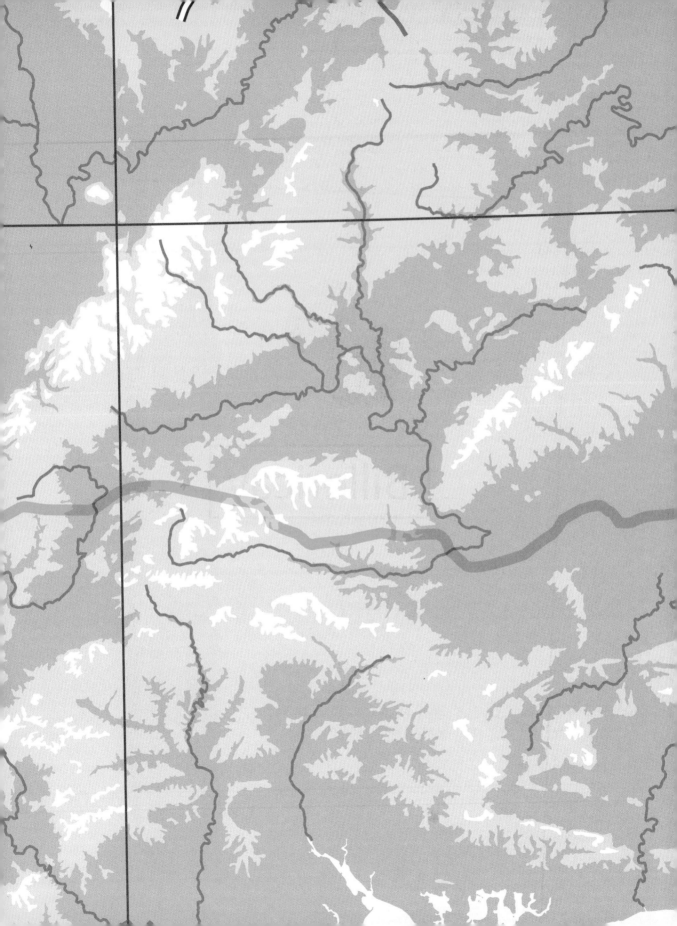

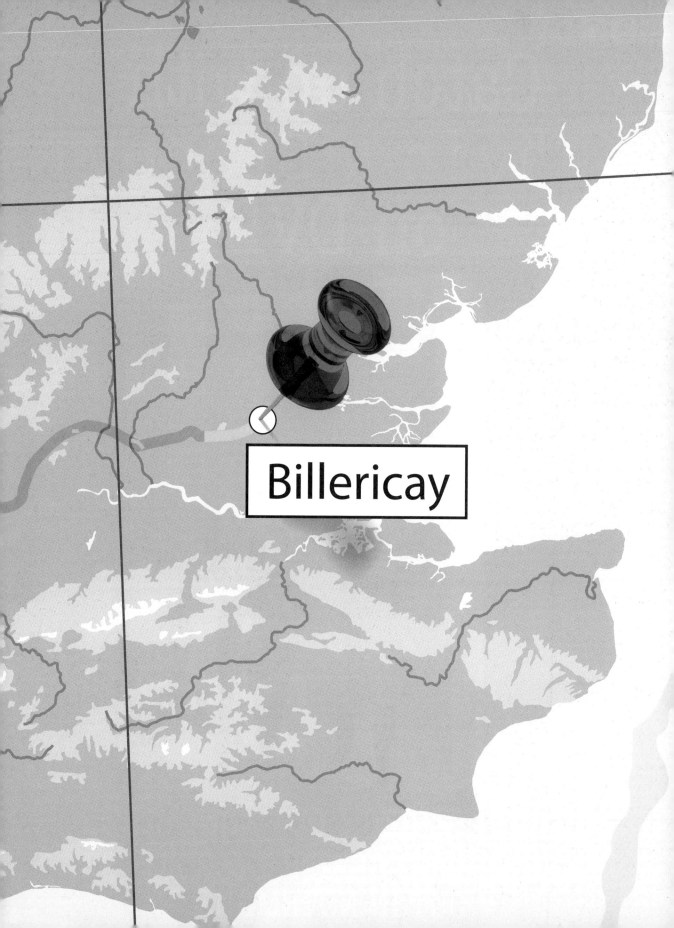

Billericay